AFTER YOU SHOOT

Your gun's hot.
The perp's not.
Now what?

Don't convict yourself.

Alan Korwin

BLOOMFIELD PRESS
Scottsdale, Arizona

BLOOMFIELD PRESS

4848 E. Cactus #505-440 • Scottsdale, AZ 85254
602-996-4020 Office • 602-494-0679 Fax
1-800-707-4020 Order Hotline

GunLaws.com

ISBN-10: 1-889632-26-0
ISBN-13: 978-1-889632-26-1

Photograph of the author by Michael Ives
Cover design by Ralph Richardson

ATTENTION
Clubs, Organizations, Libraries, Firearms Training Instructors,
Schools, Educators and all interested parties:
Contact the publisher for information on quantity discounts!

Every gun owner needs this book—
"It doesn't make sense to own a gun and not know the rules."

Visit our website for updates and other information
concerning this book and our entire line of products.

Printed and bound in the United States of America
at Color House Graphics, Grand Rapids, Michigan

First Edition

Table of Contents

Disclaimer

The different physical circumstances of any self-defense incident are a real problem with a book like this. Advice for your home will not hold steady for the street or your car. Here you get some general discussion of issues that interest many Americans. It's an exercise in free speech, to discuss and consider matters of great concern to society, not a blueprint for the use of deadly force.

This book is not legal advice, and I'm not a lawyer, I'm a First Amendment guy, a writer. Every use-of-force case *will* be different, count on it. Virtually all the writings on this subject point that out, and the applicability of this book's content to your situation may be a good, bad or a terrible match. *The risks are yours and yours alone.* Remember that before you drop the hammer.

Understand that this book cuts way against the grain, challenges long-held assumptions, takes on several previously unrecognized or marginalized paradoxes and spotlights them, introduces some completely new paradigms, takes corrupt or questionable elements of the judicial system to task, and has already caused some controversy. If I succeed it will change some fundamental thinking, including possibly some of your own. All of this is being done with copious caveats that no one agrees, and that when your butt is on the line, all bets are off and your fate is terribly unpredictable regardless of your actions or preparations. Any advice you take from this book, any lawyer, your buddies, the police or anywhere

4

else you take at your own peril. Life, like this book, comes without guarantees.

Missing from this book are the endless discussions about personal effects on you and those close to you after a shooting. You may feel elation, relief, depression, mood swings, sleeplessness, stress-related effects or nothing special at all, and wonder why. Your community may embrace you as a hero, reject you as a villain, taunt and ridicule your kids and family enough to make you move.

The media may be on you at every turn, biased, twisted, seeking to sensationalize your survival, characterize you as a criminal and the criminal as a poor victim, try you in the court of popular opinion regardless of facts or any shred of evidence or human decency. Your life may never go back to what it was, or it may. You'll have to learn about all that elsewhere. This book just deals with protecting yourself legally, after you survive a felony assault or murder attempt.

Do not judge, adopt or act upon any part of this book without reading the other parts, since they often conflict with each other and offer disparate and sometimes incompatible advice. Such is the nature of this life or death subject. Only a fool would rely on this book without also studying the subject from other sources.

See our website for changes, updates, and inevitable adjustments and new thoughts on this volatile subject:

GunLaws.com

Acknowledgments

An awful lot of people spoke with me and offered advice on the way to completing this book. Some are named within, others contributed to my understanding of the subject, and others simply offered moral support and encouragement as I plodded on with what became an increasingly tough project. Foolish me, I thought this would be an easy effort. Without the help and support of so many friends and professionals it would have been an impossible dream. Thank you for being there for me.

Alan Gottlieb, Barrett Tillman, Becky Blanton, Bill Davison, Bill Montgomery, Bob Bennett, Bob Blackmer, Bob Dowlut, Bob Levy, Brian Borrelli, Bill Davison, Bruce Blumberg, Bruce Eimer, Bruce Feder, Charles Heller, Cheryl Korwin, Chris Bird, Christopher Conte, Chuck Cunningham, Chuck Michel, Clint Bolick, Dave Hardy, Dave Kenick, Dave Kopel, David Marhoffer, Duke Schecter, Eric Cartridge, Erin Simpson, Eugene Volokh, Evan Nappen, Fred Dahnke, Gary Christensen, Gary Marbut, Ignatius Piazza, Irving Korwin, Jeff Snyder, Joey Hamby, John Buttrick, John Frazer, Keith Manning, Ken Hanson, Ken Rineer, Kevin Jamison, Kurt Krause, Landis Aden, Larry Pratt, Larry Tahler, Marc MacYoung, Marc Victor, Mark Barnes, Mark Moritz, Marty Hayes, Massad Ayoob, Michael Kielsky, Mike Anthony, Mitch Vilos, Nick Dranias, Paul Heubl, Rachel Alexander, Richard Korwin, Rick Mackey, Sandy Froman, Scott Bach, Sean Healy, Stefan Tahmassebi, Steve Twist, Terry Allison, Thomas Baker, Tim Lynch, Timothy Forshey, Tom Givens, Tyler Korwin, Walt Cleveland, Wayne Anthony Ross, Wayne Northcutt, and several who must remain nameless. And as for you, Richard Stevens, you know what you did, and you can be as proud of it as you know I am to know you.

The *Adnarim* Statement
(Pronounced ad-NA-rim, same accent as *Miranda*)

"I'm interested in cooperating and will exercise my right to remain silent after reading this statement. Please do not attempt to violate my rights in this regard. *I want to speak with my attorney.* I respectfully ask you to honor this without any purpose of evasion and insist my lawyer be present prior to and during any questioning without exception.

"I refuse consent to any search of my person, papers, premises, vehicle, immediate location or effects. I invoke my rights under the 2nd, 4th, 5th, 6th, 8th, 9th, 10th and 14th Amendments to the U.S. Constitution and any applicable state or federal laws. If you Mirandize me and ask if I'll speak without my attorney present the answer is no. Thank you for your cooperation, and may I have a glass of water please."

Adnarim Statement Part Two
(For attorneys)

"Hello, 911? I'm attorney George Victory and my client has just survived an assault. An ambulance and police are needed immediately at location X. I'm enroute there now myself." Click.

Adnarim Statement Part Three
(Ten words for 911)

"I've just been attacked.
Send an ambulance and police to (location)."
Hang up. Call your lawyer. Wait.

CHAPTER ZERO
Who you gonna call?

Where does it say that after a legitimate self-defense shooting you should call 911 and make a confession? Or make any statements at all into a police voice recorder?

Oh, wait a minute—most lawyers who advise calling 911 also advise that you only say some certain things and not others. In other words, they counsel you to make some carefully prepared statements that will affect you (hopefully) in predetermined (premeditated?) ways. Don't be truthful and just spill your guts—that will hurt you, they say. Just say certain things designed to help them help you get off, and nothing else. Can that be right?

But then, most lawyers do recognize that you will be in such an agitated state after a shooting, and having just survived mortal combat, that your chances of blurting out all sorts of unintended incriminating things is huge, so they also counsel you to "just shut up." Don't say anything. Anything you say can *and will* be used against you. That might be especially true for anything the police recorded you saying, you think?

The U.S. Supreme Court, in its famous *Miranda v. Arizona* decision back in 1966 (384 U.S. 436), said you have the right to remain silent. Well, do you or don't you? They did not say you have the right to remain silent after you call 911 and make a statement into a police recorder, that can *and will* be used against you.

The High Court said you have the right to an attorney. They didn't say you have the right to an attorney later. The Constitution says, and American people believe and operate on the virtually sacred principle, that the Fifth Amendment protects you against self-incrimination.

So it occurred to me, after thinking about this logically for a while, that the advice on what to do after a self-defense shooting is inconsistent at best, and horrendous and incriminating at worst. It is self-contradictory, paradoxical, illogical, a threat to your liberty. It is.

Mention this to lawyers though, as I have, or to anyone in a position of authority like police, judges, prosecutors, educators and trainers and they're pretty clear. You better call 911 right away. It will go badly for you if you don't. It will be used against you in court. Failure to obey the state's unwritten rule and call the state and record yourself at the most stressful moment of your entire life will be used as evidence, or at least a clear implication of your guilt, regardless of any guilt you might have.

That strikes me as flat-out wrong, but what do I know.

And I better be wrong about that, because otherwise, the idea that you have the right to remain silent, and the right to an attorney, is false. If anything you say can *and will* be used against you—but you are required to speak up right after an incident—then there is no justice in the justice system. You are required to potentially implicate yourself in a capital murder case. Failure to potentially implicate yourself implicates' you too. That's not good.

As it turns out, there is no requirement in law to call 911 after a self-defense shooting. In fact, a self-defense shooting, if it is justified, is not even a crime. Now, you won't know it's not a crime until the smoke clears, your ears stop ringing, and the authorities reach a decision about your fate, possibly years later. But dialing 911 and recording yourself is not a requirement under any self-defense law in the nation. It can't be. The elements of self defense stretch back for millennia. Written American law on self defense stretches back for centuries. Dialing 911 is a brand-new invention.*

And that's why this book is here. The paradox of calling 911 but remaining silent screams for, if not resolution, profound examination. How can you best protect yourself from a false charge with a death penalty attached, and behave as a decent citizen who just survived a lethal assault by a murderous felon?

I'm not giving legal advice—I can't—I'm not a lawyer and I'm not qualified by any measure. But as a writer, with the First Amendment there filling my sails, I can certainly cruise a social situation and expound upon it, and expound I shall.

As a fine point, the *Miranda* protections of silence and an attorney apply *after* an arrest, which is when they "read you your rights." In principle though, it seems to me those concepts should apply at all times. Certainly, your Fifth Amendment rights against incriminating yourself cloak you every minute of your life in this country. *Miranda* is just window dressing from a constitutional point of view.

As a final kick in the guts—tell me exactly where in our constitutional framework we find rationale for *them* to read *us* our rights, and not the other way around?

The contradictions in the machinery of a self-defense aftermath are blatant. It's up to people with a greater effect on the subject than I to eventually sort this all out. It will fall to someone whose life is on the line, both immediately before a shooting and for a long while afterwards, to clarify some of the darker corners of this box in American jurisprudence. But it seems to have fallen to me, out of curiosity, familiarity with the subject, a passion for exposition, a tenacious pursuit of fairness and an unabashed desire to feed my family to unravel this quagmire, and lay out the pieces for the world to ponder.

* In 1968, AT&T announced its plans to establish a universal emergency phone number, selecting 911 for a variety of reasons. Discussions of establishing such a system date back to at least 1957. By 1979 about a quarter of the nation had 911 service, growing to half the nation in 1987. Today an estimated 96% of the U.S. has 911 service. It has been said that police in some southern border towns have removed the 911 signs from their squad cars, because drug cartels were stealing them, thinking they were Porsches.

CHAPTER ONE

*Your gun's hot, the perp's not,
now what?*

Call 911.

Say, "I was in fear for my life."

Say, "I thought he would kill me."

Say, "I want a lawyer."

Ask for an ambulance, because someone's been shot.

And don't say *anything*.

That's the common wisdom floating around, on what to do after you've saved your life with gunfire against a dangerous violent criminal assailant bent on murdering you.

It doesn't even make sense, but that's the common wisdom. Say this, say that, and don't say anything.
Well, which is it?

After reading all those books and taking all those classes on gun safety, gun gear, gun fighting, self defense, armed tactics and strategy, concealed carry, quick draw, stopping power, point shooting, cover and concealment, now what? You dropped the hammer, a felony perp (you think) is lying at your feet bleeding on your carpet. Who you gonna call? What do you do?

We're going to assume throughout this book that you were involved in what police call a "clean shoot" or a "good shoot." You were absolutely blameless, completely innocent, pure as the driven snow, minding your own business at a place you had every right to be, did nothing to instigate the assault. Thanks God, you're alive.

The assailant was deliberately and with premeditation committing a felonious lethal assault on you at the moment of the shooting. It may be hard or impossible to establish those facts—it typically is—but we're going to assume a situation where that's what actually happened.

It's the exact kind of event that is 100% perfectly justified, and that a reasonable person hopes never happens. You saved your life at a moment when you had no choice if you were going to survive, and had every right by law and the morality of the universe to do so.

If you're even the slightest bit less innocent than that, all bets are off. If you owed the perp money, or knew the person in any way, the shoot isn't *perfectly* clean. If you're perfectly clean but just came out of a nightclub at 2 a.m., that's less clean than sitting at home. Any complicating factor and your hurt level goes up. We're only talking here about every gun owner's realistic concern: "What do I do if I have to shoot to save my life through absolutely no fault of my own?"

A clean shoot and a shoot that looks clean are different. A ski-masked home invader shot in your bedroom after a break-and-enter may be as perfectly clean as an armed robber dropped on a late-night street corner, but the police must treat these differently. Maybe you should indeed speak up, cautiously, at home, to allay suspicion and maintain goodwill. Maybe that's less true on the street corner. How suspicious do the cops seem, or is their nonchalance a Columbo act? Are they just trying to trick you to speak so they can convict you more easily?

The dead masked home invader shot by a home owner in her nightgown may be the most self-evident example of self defense known. On the street, in your vehicle, while hiking a trail—a shooting is something you can only hope will be found to be self defense, even if it perfectly is.

The answer to the gun-show question I hear from time to time—a threatening scene described and the query, "Should I have shot him?" is an emphatic *no*. You're standing there. That's proof you didn't face imminent death, needed to justify your shot. Of course, you didn't know that when the apparent threat appeared, but you do wonder about it for the rest of your life.

But even if a shoot was slightly less than perfectly pure, even if all you did was accidentally shoot your lawyer friend right in the face with a shotgun blast at close range while hunting with a bunch of witnesses, what's your next move? Or what if you fired to protect a clean-cut stranger on the street who was about to be gunned down by some disheveled vagabond. And what if it turned out—despite all appearances and your best guess at that instant—you actually took out an undercover FBI agent about to shoot the most wanted shoot-on-sight suitcase-nuke-carrying islamist jihadi on the planet. What do you do next?

Slowly, dimly, you start to recognize that all your books and study are basically about *before* an incident. That's why you shot clean and only hit your intended target with lethal accuracy. What do you say and do at the scene, when they're stringing yellow crime-scene tape?

"Say nothing." Everyone's heard that.

So, do you just stand there in mute autistic silence and walk around like a robot? "Good evening, sir, what happened here?" Silence. "Is this your home?" Silence. "Who are you?" Silence. "Hey Sarge, we're going to have to run this guy in, he's being completely uncooperative." Silence. "He looks guilty to me." Silence.

Or do you say something. *Anything*.

Of course you say something. *Everyone* says *something*. Reports from people in that situation consistently indicate they are *overflowing* with a burning desire to talk. What should your words be? Should you decide beforehand or just go with the flow? If you decide beforehand, is that premeditation? Will it work against you?

Whatever you can think of to say, and there will be plenty—your mind racing, blood pressure soaring, adrenaline clouding your brain, shaking your body— enormous pressure brought to bear to get you to talk, thoughts scattered... and if you talk you say things you're not supposed to say "that can *and will* be used *against* you in a court of law. Do you understand the statement I've just read to you?" How do you prevent that?

This book provides some ideas about these questions, but *there are no hard and fast answers.* In all my research, *no one* offered the same advice. None of the RKBA experts agree on *precisely* what to do, and some completely disagree with each other. Some of the so-called experts—and even some attorneys—are anything but expert (based on the witheringly stupid and self-contradictory advice they offered). A fine justice system that is. Some rejected every basic concept I'm putting forward. Who knows. Maybe they're right.

But there are in fact some *real* experts, and they do have a pretty good idea of an appropriate course of action. And they've been through this a lot, a real lot. Enough to have come up with a plan that is tried and true, time tested, and used uniformly across the country, approved of by city councils, internal affairs departments and the courts. And if it's good enough for them—the police officers—maybe it's good enough for you. Maybe that's where we should start.

As you digest this synthesis of their ideas, and some new ideas, you'll see that some make sense. You'll also see that some "experts" don't make very much sense at all. Those are mainly the ones who say, "Say nothing and ask for a lawyer," which is itself a contradiction in terms—concepts we'll examine in these pages. And saying, "I need to speak with my attorney," is critically important to say, since it has virtually magic power in protecting you legally. Or at least it's supposed to.

And as to the common-wisdom humor of, "Call the police, call an ambulance, call for a pizza, and see who gets there first," that's dumb gallows humor. Author Jeff Snyder, who wrote the stunning time-tested essay

Nation of Cowards, says that sort of humor hurts us in the public eye and he's got a point. And yes, the pizza gets there first about half the time.

The whole matter is extra complex because, in the minutes and hours and days and even years after the most transforming event you may ever face in your life, you won't be exactly following some clear prescription you read about somewhere. You make your moves, whatever they are, and you get to see where the cards fall. You simply do not know what you're going to say and do ahead of time, just like on a first date.
No one does.

So even the best advice will miss the mark because the facts of every occurrence will differ. Every successful self-defense incident is unique—different time, place, surroundings, different actors and different responders. The only consistency is in the preferred sequence of events—bad guy loses, you win, aftermath happens.

The same way you can't just sit here now holding this book and predict exactly when and where and how you may ever face the shootout, you can't begin to guess about the aftermath. It will become the greatest story ever told (for you). And *that's* one of your greatest risks, not the kind of ammo you use and which of your many guns you put it in that day (which you've no doubt given *plenty* of thought).

If you remember anything from this book, let it be these
NEW SAFETY RULES FOR SELF DEFENSE:

1. If you ever shoot in self defense you must then defend yourself against execution for murder.

2. When you drop the hammer plan to cash in your life savings for your lawyer's retainer. Avoid this unless your life depends on it.

3. Sometimes the innocent get decent treatment, sometimes they don't.

4. It's always better to avoid a gunfight than to win one.

5. If innocent life doesn't immediately depend on it, don't shoot. And if it does, don't miss.

Your gun's hot, the perp's not, now what?

CHAPTER TWO
Learn from the pros

Let's see what the police do.

They're *real* experts at this, with plenty of experience.

Police officers involved in a shooting actually *don't* say a thing.

At least at first. Officers involved in a shooting are removed from all outside contact by their handlers, for two weeks, with pay.* The handlers (not the shooters) tell the press and anyone else who asks that the officer "has been placed on administrative leave, with pay." Not a thing is outside the team-controlled environment. Nice. It's a good start.

No one questions this, or suggests they are hiding anything, or tries to get around the two-week black out. It's widely considered normal, no big deal. The "with pay" part is very important. It implies, "There's nothing wrong here, the officer acted properly, and is getting a much need stress-relief and debriefing period that any normal person needs and would want and deserves."

If that's good enough for Officer Friendly and the entire police force nationwide, it is probably good enough for you, just an average innocent citizen.

(In fairness, homicide and internal affairs are on the scene right quick investigating an officer-involved shooting. Officers can, like you, refuse to speak with homicide, but must speak with IA. However, the IA conversations cannot be used as evidence, just as your dialog with your attorney is privileged and cannot be used. Everything is held internally for a long while.)

That procedure is at the heart of one rational principle— no sense in reinventing the wheel: *A citizen-involved shooting should follow similar procedures to an officer-involved shooting.* It doesn't, but it should.

It's all about equal treatment under the law. No discrimination based on your lot in life. It's about fairness, and blind justice. It's the right thing to do.

The handlers (not the officer) then issue a statement... no one speaks up or *says* anything (it's that common-wisdom thing again). They issue a statement—in writing—in collaboration with an army of lawyers and teammates (who you pay for through your taxes by the way). The officer shooter vouches for the statement, and probably signs it, but all the public gets to see is a press-release version. The document itself is carefully protected by the handlers.

At the press conference, if there even is one, two weeks later when things have settled down, the officer may not even be present, and if present, stands autistically still in the background and says nothing. The PIO (public information officer, the police-department mouthpiece) does the talking. The pack-media's cameras click away like mad. Maybe the Chief or some underling makes statements. The officer does not. The officer stands behind the written statement, with all its words carefully in a row, blessed by the people behind the curtain. There's no telling what might slip out of the officer's mouth (or yours) if it opens up and yaks.

This methodology is approved by the police themselves. The judges and prosecutors and defense attorneys they work with, all the lawyers they work with, every city council in the nation has blessed this as the correct way to handle the "first responder." The perp (never called the victim) goes to the morgue.

It sounds like a good, safe, justice-oriented approach, doesn't it? We certainly wouldn't want to suggest the police have civil rights that exceed our own, right? No one suggests that this approach hides anything or compromises justice, correct? The cool presumption of innocence is maintained with excruciating precision as long as nothing overtly suspicious develops.

If that's good enough for the police, it's good enough for you. That's one of the main paradigm shifts in this book—*you deserve to be treated in the same fair manner as the police are treated*. It's tried and true, time tested, and used uniformly across the country. It's a good starting point.

Unfortunately, prevailing thought doesn't go that way. Police look at each other (and look after each other) as innocent employees to serve and protect (errant video recordings notwithstanding). You, all too often you're just another shooting suspect to investigate and convict. Many times that's fair. Many times not.

Anyone who thinks the public as a rule should not be entitled to the exact same protections our hired police force is entitled to needs to explain why, and what level of diminished protection the public should labor under or be subjected to by, well, who exactly?

:::

Part of the problem for you is that they (the police) have a team, and you don't. They have handlers, you don't. Their team is on site right away. Yours, maybe only one single person, might be sleeping and unwilling to get out of bed. This is erroneously called blind justice.

They have thought it all through ahead of time, you haven't. No one calls their planning premeditation. For you, maybe less accepting. Your preparation may be no greater than the countless boxes of 135-grain copper-jacketed hollowpoints you bought in 9mm (a hopelessly lightweight round?). Your preparation may be no greater than that you have just started reading this book, which didn't even exist until late 2010.

If you're like too many folks in the small club of people who have legitimately fired a gun to save a life, you probably met your first lawyer the day after you pulled the trigger. That may not be the best plan, you think?

And your crisis-response team, well, you don't have one. Only the authorities are collecting evidence, taking pictures and measurements, making witness lists, asking questions and taking notes. If you had a PI (a private investigator) on your team, there would be evidence and information and photographs gathered by you for your own use. That could be handy, you think?

Now, if you *do* have a team, say, you're from Beverly Hills and a shooting occurs, the result is very different. Your lawyers (plural), who arrived there first and are working the scene with their own investigator, talk to the police department's second responders (*you* are the first responder) and they make a deal.

Instead of "a trip downtown" you have dinner at home, and no charges are filed. Hey, you didn't do anything wrong—shooting a person in legitimate self defense is not a crime. It is honorable, righteous, decent, saves an innocent, eliminates a felon in the commission of a felony, it's the right and moral thing to do. Police even have a friendly name for it. They call it "the good riddance factor." A good guy is alive, a bad guy is not, that's a good thing. It is *so* not a crime that the FBI doesn't even keep track of the statistics (but activists say they ought to, and scholars have researched it thoroughly.)**

For most of you, even after reading this book, you'll coast along at the mercy of fate, the state and the moment. You'll figure you can prepare later. Spending money to "have" a lawyer will land on the back burner. Maybe you'll actually finish this book and remember some of it if you ever find yourself in your hour of need. That's probably OK, because the chances of ending up in a horrific fight to the death that leaves you alive and some other guy dead are remote. Just carry your gun, plenty of ammo, and *feel* safe. Because you probably are. Probably. Sure, the right mindset to cultivate is, "a lawyer gets my life savings if I fire," but sometimes, the scene ends with a pat on the back and no charges filed. Sometimes.

Actually, the pat on the back, "no bill," "turn down," decision to not prosecute is more common than you might realize, but it is not something to encourage people to expect. It certainly isn't the safe way to approach the subject.

* In an officer-involved shooting, there is a deep presumption by responding officers that the officer-shooter acted properly—which a citizen might deserve (innocent unless proven guilty) but really does not get in the same way. This is understandable, since the majority of officer responses to a call of shots fired involve a criminal perpetrator and possible mortal danger to the responding officers. At the scene of an officer-involved shooting, it's typical for Internal Affairs to do an immediate "walk-through" with the officer to reconstruct the situation as closely as possible. They seek to establish facts, timing, distances, and other exculpatory evidence to build a good case for the officer, which a citizen would never be compelled to do. The results of the walk-through are for internal purposes only and are inadmissible in court, which is why police freely comply (and how IA was able to establish such a procedure). The information is used to establish the innocence of the officer. If during the walk-through it starts becoming apparent that something is amiss, that the officer might be open to charges, the game changes, the officer lawyers up, and all bets are off. For a civilian-involved shooting, evidence is typically compiled to establish someone's guilt, the exact opposite goal, and you the suspect are in the spotlight.

** Thirteen scholarly studies have found between 700,000 and 3.4 million DGUs (defensive gun uses) per year. The different counts are a function of different definitions of a DGU (within the prior year or prior years, multiple assailants, gun mentioned, drawn, fired, etc.) different respondent sets (homeowners, outdoors, age groups, etc.), and different time periods. The highest figure comes from the Justice Dept. study under president Clinton. The studies can be found in the book *Armed, New Perspectives on Gun Control* by Kleck and Kates, available at gunlaws.com.

CHAPTER THREE
Your attorney

You do have an attorney, right?

Most people with guns do not.

What does it mean, exactly, to "have" an attorney?

At the same time you bought all your guns, 5,000 rounds of ammo for each, took some classes and read a handful of good books on gun laws, tactics and strategy, you found yourself a good attorney, right?

It seems most people who own thousands of rounds of ammo in every caliber known to man never think about this gunfighting step. It's well past time to go there. (You might also want to consider getting some bandages, another severely overlooked aspect of civilian gun ownership.) A meeting with a lawyer and a case or two of ammo cost about the same thing. Admittedly, though, ammo typically lasts longer.

So how do you find a lawyer who knows guns and you can trust? First, stop making lawyer jokes. Second, think about solving this *now*. Shopping for a lawyer when you desperately need one (just like shopping for a gun) is the wrong time to go shopping.

Firearms-friendly, firearms-savvy lawyers are out there. You can find them in several ways. Recommendations work. If you don't have a friend, or a friend who knows a proper lawyer, find your state bar association, or a yellow pages, and start making calls. That's common advice. I don't like it.

Instead, find your state gun-rights organizations. You'll find them all listed at gunlaws.com, under the National Directory button, or just Google around for it. You should put this book down for six minutes and go join a group, like, now. Do it. I'll wait.

Joining gives you *connections*. It makes getting answers easier. Members are treated like, well, members, not outsiders. Joining also helps protect your right to keep your guns and ammo in the first place. For self defense you're better off belonging to a state group. Be a big sport. Join your state group and a national group.

Folks in your local gun-rights groups know or can find local attorneys for you to call. But that's a pretty scary call for the average government-schooled person to make. Has this book made you eager to make that call? Right. Schools don't prepare you for dealing with serious real-world players. Conspiracy theorists say that's the plan.

It's an easy call to make though, when you know how. Here's how.

You tell the secretary who answers, or the lawyer if you're lucky enough to get that person on the line (or even the answering machine), "Hello, I'd like to make an appointment for a *consultation*. I have some questions about gun ownership—is that something you could help me with?" That will get the ball rolling, and likely get the attorney on the phone.

On that initial phone call you scope out the person to see if you'll be wasting *your* time. "I'm looking for an attorney who has experience in criminal-defense work involving firearms. Would that describe you?" Be quiet. Let the person speak. Listen hard. Take notes.

Ask followup questions that naturally flow from the opening dialog. The lawyer should naturally ask if you're in some sort of trouble, but if not, you need to bring it up. "I'm not in any sort of difficulty, but as a gun owner, I think it would be prudent for me to have a relationship with a good attorney just in case." Be quiet again. Let the person speak. Listen hard.

Be sure to ask, "So what are our state guidelines for using deadly force in self defense?" That's a litmus test that will reveal if you've got a good guy or a blowhard. If you like what you're hearing, ask how much a one-hour office visit will cost. It should be somewhere in low to mid three figures.

Some good attorneys, if they think you sound like a good prospective client, might not charge for an initial consultation. But don't let that be a deciding factor for you, and it's not an advantage. Commit now, to yourself, to pay for a meeting, which is better. Instead of a freebie and a loose relationship, you become a genuine paying client. This is good.

If the lawyer asks what kind of piece you carry you can pretty well guess you've got a decent connection. Some might mention (brag?) they're a member of this group or that, which doesn't hurt. You do *not* want a real-estate or personal-injury lawyer, no matter how badly they want your business. Be discriminating. Lawyers are as specific as gun types. You need the right one. Bite the bullet and set the appointment at a time convenient for you.

During your paid one-hour consultation you get to know each other. You should prepare and ask every gun question you can think of. Can't think of any? For starters, ask about the fee structure. Use the question list in the back of this book. Some of the questions you need answered are real pedal-to-the-metal issues— because if you shoot in self defense you could face 20 years to life, starting at two in the morning on a dark and blustery night. Didn't think about that when you bought all your hollowpoint ammo, did you?

Don't spend too much time like a gun bubba talking hunting and gun types, although a little for rapport is fine. Steer clear of theoretical questions like, "Does ammo type matter?" and instead get concrete. "Have you ever heard of a case where ammo type mattered?"

You'll learn a lot. It's fun. Bring a lawyer-style yellow pad in a leatherette pad holder and take a ton of notes. Makes you feel powerful and *connected*. You're building a team. This is good.

When your time's up, you shake hands and pay up. Either write a check right there (giving you a few extra moments for extra chatter), or pay in cash. Ask, "Is cash OK?" Cash is good.

Lawyers like cash, just like everyone. No wondering if the check is good. No waiting to collect. Less paperwork. Maybe not even bookkeeping, which of course violates government rules (and has been known to occur, but it's not *your* violation). Tells you something about the person too, especially if the firm has partners. If you went to this meeting with friends—a very smart move—you can split the fee. And the lawyer sees multiple potential clients.

Now put your new attorney's cards (plural) in your wallet, glovebox, briefcase, desk and spouse's hand. Now you can say those magic, connected, power-broker, bragging-rights phrases. "I need to speak to *my* lawyer." "He's my attorney." "Let me ask my attorney and see what he thinks." And of course, "My attorney says blah blah yada yada do wha ditty ditty."

Now when you meet the police at the door, (with your gun reloaded and ready nearby—no way to know if the perp might reanimate), you greet them with your ID and *your* attorney's card in hand, like a good neighbor. Now instead of saying, "I want an attorney," you say, "I'm waiting for my attorney."

If you think about it, asking for "an" attorney is totally wrong. You're asking people who've arrived to arrest and prosecute you to provide you with a defense. They are the *last* people to ask for an attorney. Asking police who arrived to investigate a shooting to provide an attorney is an act of ultimate unprepared ignorant desperation.

Having an attorney puts your mind at ease, and has some fringe benefits. Now that you've paid good cash money for a mere sit down, this person is your ally, on your team, part of your support structure, and with a little luck and watering, soon to be a friend. That one paid consultation lasts, well, forever. As long as the two of you walk the Earth, you have a relationship.

This is a relationship to nurture. You are now in an elite category known as "paying client," however small in the scheme of things. You can probably get a real brief question or two answered on the phone without charge. Exercise this valuable asset with discretion. Or just pay the bill once in a while, to keep the relationship fresh.

In the not-too-distant future, call with a question that you not only need answered, but that helps the attorney to stay up to speed. *Be your lawyer's ally.* "Hey George, does that new law affect my AR-15? Do you understand that new carry law they're debating?" Know the number so you can tell him if needed, or better yet, describe some arcane part and ask if you have it right. "Will my permit remain good if they change the training requirement?" This is a good conversation to have, and keep it short and sweet. Expect longer discussions to include a bill in the mail, which is OK (and you can again split with your buddies, who are also part of your team). You need to feed an attorney, and attorneys need to feed themselves.

Invite George to a shoot. "I have tickets to that machine-gun day out at the range, and I thought you might like to join me." Even if he doesn't go, you know he'll brag to his friends about that. Better yet, "I'm going to the Federalist Society seminar here in town with Supreme Court Justice Alito, do you want to join me?"

Bird-dog information when you can, maybe by email, "The state rifle association annual meeting is coming up, might be some potential clients there for you, would you like to go as my guest?" Best fifty bucks you'll ever spend, and you're walking on air when you introduce your well-dressed friend as your attorney. At dinner, everyone picks his brain, and he feels special. Don't overdo it, but act as if your attorney is a good trusted friend, because your attorney should be. Including people in activities makes them feel good. The fee you paid should be a two-way street with a lot of mileage on it.

Your attorney

CHAPTER FOUR
An example illustrates

"Hello, I'm vice president Dick Cheney and I've called this national press conference to announce that I just now innocently shot my lawyer in the face at close range with this here shotgun while we were hunting."

Experts agree this is not the correct approach.

Despite this the "news" media (decidedly *not* experts) got apoplectic, hammering and clamoring insanely for the vice president of the United States to behave that way. They cursed him (figuratively) for not doing so. He wisely did not, censoring himself for a while. Reporters were livid, wearing anti-rights, freedom-suppressing, agenda-driven shameful bias on their sleeves.

When was the last time you saw *any* "news" report about any shooting that treated a surviving innocent citizen nicely? I rest that case.

An interesting limit on free speech, this one is optional, self imposed and a really good idea—don't make verbal statements to authorities or anyone (except privately to your lawyer) immediately after an incident that might lead to your arrest, even if you are 101% innocent. You not only don't have an obligation to incriminate yourself, you have constitutional protection and a moral obligation *against* incriminating yourself. It's called the Fifth Amendment. The Supreme Court put it plainly. *You have the right to remain silent*. Do it. Exercise your right, judiciously, with help of counsel.

If you ever find yourself in a Cheney-style debacle, do *not* grab your cell phone to call and talk with fair and balanced, even handed, accurate, knowledgeable, moral, unbiased, gun-friendly, accurate, trustworthy, ethical, decent, reliable, accurate and temperate reporters you know. Or anyone else you know, *except your lawyer* (not "a" lawyer).

Recognize, however, that a phone is an integral part of self-defense gear—sidearm, ammo, holster, cell phone.

Imagine it's late, dark and you're alone at home asleep in a good neighborhood. You're aroused from a dream by the distinct sound of breaking glass from somewhere down the hall. In your pajamas, you slip on your slippers, take your fully loaded cocked-and-locked 1911-A Colt Officer's Model .45 caliber sidearm with the new custom grips, trigger job and tritium night sights from a secret compartment behind your nightstand, and walk inside to investigate.

As soon as you turn the corner, a scruffy-looking stranger backlit by your kitchen nightlight comes right at you with something in hand—and next thing you know you hear a shot whiz by your ear. Your adrenaline was flowing and then skyrockets but you coolly snap off the thumb safety like you've done a thousand times before and fire at the center of mass just as you were trained. The person wobbles but keeps coming. You get an immediate live-action test result on the one-shot-stop theory. You find out it's just a theory.

Gun-safety-rule number 62 pops into mind. "Anything worth shooting is worth shooting twice—ammo is cheap, innocent life isn't." Bang, you double tap an instant later. The figure still presses forward, and now you're totally scared to death. Suddenly, you recall gun safety rule number 162. "When in doubt, empty the magazine." You fire until the gun is unloaded and the slide locks back, and you try firing a few times after that too. You have no extra magazines in your PJs and you stand, transfixed, stunned, ears ringing madly, unable to move.

The stranger, suspended upright in mid-charge by the impact of your carefully selected 230-grain +P jacketed hollowpoint personal-protection ammo, drops like a wet sack of potatoes, while your ears continue to ring wildly from the noise. Switching on the light, you can tell it's the annoying big kid from down the block who you've argued with before and never trusted.

Do everything possible to avoid ever being in this situation.

Recognize also, however, that this happens with some frequency, worldwide. Remember, scholarly estimates of defensive gun use uniformly find hundreds of thousands to millions of DGU incidents in the U.S. annually, most of which do not involve firing the gun... its presence is usually sufficient to disengage most confrontations.

The intruder charging an armed homeowner is the exception not the rule, but it does happen. Another perp might stop, make nice, and attempt a take away (of your gun). He might pull a distraction to pull a gun on you. Or he might just go for his gun while you have the drop on him, figuring you'll never shoot, or he'll shoot first, or you'll miss with your first shot, especially as he sidesteps (a great tactical move by the way). Maybe he figures he's not going to prison even if it kills him. He might smile, back off, and make for the door. He might claim he's drunk and walked into the wrong house, which could be true. Some perps will claim to be police and try to command you—now *there's* a terrifying scenario. The varieties are endless. No two events are ever the same. Have you ever walked your home to check the lines of sight? Are there any really safe shots you could take indoors there? How good a shot are you in your PJs right after you wake from a deep sleep?

Eventually, police *will* be on the scene—as normal—well after the event occurs. They don't draw their guns. They draw chalk lines when you're gone. You've heard it before, or it's time to hear it now: "When seconds count, the police are just minutes away." The police know this. The media, with typically ignorant inaccuracy call those officers first responders. Nonsense. You and you alone are the first responder, even if the perp wins.

This part takes an instant. Shooting your lawyer in the face is a brief experience. Stopping a home invader takes seconds. What comes next lasts for years.

CHAPTER FIVE
Dial 911 and fry
The *"Adnarim"* Statement

The situation a reasonable person works hard to avoid and sincerely hopes will never happen has happened to you. You decided to produce a firearm and shoot at another human being to save your life or the life of another innocent person. You're gasping for breath. Your gun's hot. The perp's not. Now what?

Warning: *There is no real consensus on what to do.* Some authorities object strenuously to some of what I explore or speculate upon in this book, and since each situation will be totally different, no agreement can be expected. Each situation, as it plays out, will be its own case and story. Ask batches of people for advice, as I did in developing the ideas that follow, and you'll get batches of different opinions, as I did.

The debate over what appears here will never end. It is my sincere hope you never get to add your personal experience to this chapter. Until court cases set precedent on any ideas in this book, results are wholly unpredictable and *it is you and you alone that is on the line* in order to find out. Life comes without guarantees. Remember—it's always better to avoid a gunfight than to survive one.

With your ears ringing madly from the blast of your firearm, you run through the Civilian Response Model—

1. Determine as best you can that the immediate threat has been neutralized. Scan your surroundings.

2. From cover, reload. The threat may be over, or may not be over. Accomplices may be present or planning to act. The perpetrator may reanimate. An empty gun is dangerous. Your safety and the safety of your family or other innocents should be an honest person's paramount concern at that point—not the murderous villain you just stopped. Scan for witnesses, evidence and possible other dangers as you reload.

The person with the bloody holes relinquished the right to civil treatment by acting in the way that allowed, empowered, entitled and justified you to legally shoot in the first place. Once the immediacy of your justification ends—when the perp has been neutralized—after you're sure you're physically safe for the moment—proceed to further ensure your safety, along with that of the criminal who just assaulted you.

3. Call your attorney without further delay, very briefly describe the highlights of the situation, protected by the privacy of attorney-client privilege, and ask your attorney what to do because you're traumatized and in no condition to do so yourself—while realizing that you have started the billing clock and incurred the sizeable retainer you've both already discussed. Your attorney should then *immediately* call 911 for an ambulance and a police response, while rushing to the scene to help defend you, as you've previously discussed, the same as the police would do. Your attorney's call to 911 prevents you from blurting out agitated unintentional adrenaline-clouded statements into a police recorder, "that can *and will* be used *against you.*" Most attorneys I've spoken to reject this idea. See the chapters later where they speak.

4. When police finally respond, you have your reloaded firearm in a safe place removed from the incident scene before answering the door. If you're outdoors, the sidearm should be re-holstered or secured in your vehicle, and expect the police to ask for custody of it.

5. If the police arrive before your lawyer, answer the door or greet police at the scene with your hands open and palms up, picture ID and your lawyer's card on one of them, and say, "I'm Phil Intheblank, thank God you're here." If your attorney arrived first, stand quietly in the background, let your representative do *everything*, and quietly observe. Don't agree, disagree, explain, expand, nod agreement or disagreement. Say nothing. Observe. Anything you say can *and will* be used against you. Let your attorney earn the steep fees. If you must speak, take your attorney aside and speak privately, quietly.

6. If it's just you and the man, when they start asking questions—*and they will*—you can say your name and the magic seven words: "I need to speak with my attorney." That's called ***invoking your rights*** and has legal weight. That's supposed to stop them, but it won't, but it's important to state. It creates legal protections for you. If they press on—*and they will*—you need to read them the *Adnarim* ("reverse *Miranda*") statement on the back of your lawyer's card, or just show it to them:

The *Adnarim* Statement

"I'm interested in cooperating and will exercise my right to remain silent after reading this statement. Please do not attempt to violate my rights in this regard. *I want to speak with my attorney.* I respectfully ask you to honor this without any purpose of evasion and insist my lawyer be present prior to and during any questioning without exception.

"I refuse consent to any search of my person, papers, premises, vehicle, immediate location or effects. I invoke my rights under the 2nd, 4th, 5th, 6th, 8th, 9th, 10th and 14th Amendments to the U.S. Constitution and any applicable state or federal laws. If you Mirandize me and ask if I'll speak without my attorney present the answer is no. Thank you for your cooperation, and may I have a glass of water please."

The short version of the Civilian Response Model is:

1. Make sure you're safe.

2. Reload while scanning your surroundings.

3. Call your attorney, to *immediately* call 911.

4. Secure your firearm.

5. Meet police open handed with ID and lawyer's card.

6. Read or hand over the *Adnarim* statement, if needed.

I said people disagree on what to do or say, and the steps and statements above may have already raised some questions in your own mind. I have my own concerns and make some suggestions later. Lawyers around the nation may choose to adopt this version of the *Adnarim* model and statement or not, or invent their own, or disagree completely, or do nothing (the worst approach in my opinion, even though it seems to be the most popular). No one can have a clear understanding of its implications until it ends up in court more than once. With that in mind, explore some of the thoughts I got from experts in the later chapters.

Why you should remain silent

• You will be the least capable of making coherent and consistent statements with good word choices and chronological accuracy immediately after a shooting (or other violent confrontation), even though the urge to talk will be overpowering, and *everyone* around you will encourage you to speak.

• Experience shows that a person's ability to recount events in correct order after a life-threatening trauma is terrible.

• *Every time you're asked to describe something you will do it differently*, if you make the unwise decision to start speaking. The versions won't match, and this will work against you later. You will sound like you're making things up even though you're not. That's just the way it is, the biology of it. Hey, you do that when you're not full of adrenaline and stress and just telling any old story, with no microscope up your backside examining your every inflection.

• Your veracity will be shot. The inconsistencies are a prosecutor's wet dream. "You said this, but then you said this, which one do you expect us to believe?" This is precisely why police wisely do not make statements on the scene, or verbal statements later after an officer-involved shooting. That's smart, safe, proper and a model to respect and emulate.

• The police and authorities you come in contact with will encourage you to do otherwise—they will act as your friends and try to convince you to speak. After you start talking, you have implicitly waived your right to the presence of an attorney, and everything you say can *and will* indeed be used against you. The police (in most cases) are not collecting evidence to help you get off. Maybe they should be. Maybe they should be there strictly for the defense of the innocent. Maybe schools should present a more realistic view of Officer Friendly at a "crime scene" which in a self defense is really a "crime-averted scene." Don't hold your breath.

• The main job of most shooting investigators is to corral criminals. Don't like that? Go fight city hall. Some guy is holding a smoking gun, some other guy is lying dead at his feet. What would you think? Police busy "making collars" are only indirectly working to defend the innocent, unfortunately. Police are reluctant to admit this, and may say the opposite.

:::

Speaking of opposites, and what police might deny, police are trained to react and respond differently than civilians, imagine that. A retired police officer confides:

> I was trained to think about the aftermath and how to avoid the legal issues. I love that you're being a contrarian Alan, the only way to solve things is to look at them from all angles—not just the accepted or assumed correct angle.

> Beforehand is just speculation—it's an endless game of "If this, then that." Police training around this issue was formally all about closing the loopholes and making sure you had done

enough to ensure that you would survive an inquiry. Informally the policy was, "Better to be tried by 12 than carried by 6."

We were trained to do the things we had to do to survive the courtroom—not the situation, but told when it got down to it we had to decide to live or die and deal with the courts later.

The primary progression we were taught is proof of escalation. If possible, escalate by steps. Verbal, restraint, physical force, pepper spray or dog, baton, sap, then gun. You had to prove you "did everything in your power to stop them before you were forced to use deadly force." We were taught to kill, not wound. *Never ever* go into a shooting situation to wound. That was hammered into us. *Shoot to kill.* Dead bad guys can't testify against you and lie. Cops are taught what to do in a situation to avoid prosecution and criticism—not necessarily what is the best thing for the situation. That's the whole reason six cops will jump one person—so they don't "hurt" him. But the thing people don't realize is that triggers mob reaction in the cops— most of whom are angry, scared and feeling that adrenaline rush prior to running the bad guy down. I *totally* get why cops beat up a suspect.

The thing is we received two kinds of instruction—the official version, the policy version in the manual etc., and then the "real" thing to do—the verbal "how it really works" version. That includes how to carry a "throw-down" gun, how to write up your report—all the illegal stuff cops get nailed for from time-to-time. No one will talk about that on the record and if they do the rest of the brotherhood will deny it. You'll never find those policies written down.

Post incident? Yes, we were told all the things to do to save our butt and the department's butt—we were told what would happen, what to expect, what to do, what not to do. You basically shut up, call your union rep and don't talk. You write down what happened for your own peace of mind as soon as possible afterwards, but not in an official capacity. Trauma will "erase" a lot of your memories about the event days or even hours afterward. We were told what to expect psychologically— how other officers would call us heroes although we wouldn't feel that way—a lot of how to survive the mental aspects of shooting—what to expect in terms of stress, PTSD and so on.

As I've often observed, the Al Pacino movie *Serpico*, as good as it was, didn't end routine abusive practices. The same goes for the more recent Russell Crowe flick *American Gangster*, highlighting documented internal police corruption on way massive scales, with arrests, convictions, and business as usual the following day. And of course, there are those niggling video tapes that contradict the neat stories police sometimes tell that simply don't match the evidence.

The point is, you and the authorities are at cross purposes here. From the cops' perspective, you should be as forthright and open as possible (unlike what *they* might be inclined to do behind the blue curtain). After all, if you've done nothing wrong you have nothing to hide, right? Just come clean and you'll be fine. Isn't that what you were taught in government-run grade school?

I sat through a police-led firearms-training class where the lieutenant in charge said exactly that, giving the exact opposite advice even a lousy lawyer would give you, and he knew it.

After a legitimate self-defense shooting, when the police arrive, this Lieutenant Friendly said, just tell them everything, you have nothing to fear, the justice system will protect you, since you're innocent you'll be scot-free in no time. He told this to a room full of CHL instructors, so they could pass it on to their students. Some of them raised their eyebrows higher than mine, but nobody spoke up about it in class. No sense in ticking off the police before you're even in an incident.

The lieutenant's advice is absolutely untrue and horrible. You and the police have different goals, different interests, and you are *not* on the same side in such a situation. And remember—you're not innocent until a judge or jury say you are, perhaps years later.

:::

Police often take notes by hand, on paper, and the accuracy of those notes is a great risk to you. Worse, standard police policy is to type up the handwritten notes later and destroy—yes destroy—the originals. Yes, it sure sounds like destruction of evidence, and it is. But—

Courts have *uniformly* blessed this practice. In the past when defendants could subpoena those notes it frequently helped their cases. To resolve the "problem" police do the logical thing—they quickly take those notes out of the picture. It becomes evidence you're not allowed to see, because it is legally destroyed. This is called blind justice.

Police typically come in and start "taking statements." Like Columbo, it's just routine. The idea that you have the right to remain silent is not part of that picture.

Cops arrive at the scene of a shooting pumped up, ready for shootouts or anything, it's only natural. They arrive in reasonable fear for their lives. Their number one question, "Where's the gun?"

What's the number one concern of cops who arrive on the scene of a possible crime? *Officer safety.* Secure the scene, that's secondary. They may cuff people on the spot for officer safety. Treating you with kid gloves and demure concern for your upset is not the order of the day, especially if you're somewhere not at home.

If ten people were to take notes, you'd have ten different accounts of the event. Which one is most in your favor, and which one least? To what degree do any of them reflect what actually occurred? The people listening to you—if you prattle—will have their own selective recall. Whatever feelings they have about citizen self defense will undoubtedly affect how and what is written down. Every transcription will introduce new inaccuracies.

The *Miranda* statement itself advises you not to talk with police unless your lawyer is present—but police know from long experience most people ignore that.

Maybe your first concern should be for the injured party since, not being a doctor, you don't know if the person is still alive and can be saved. If you used a 9mm the perp still might be.

The *Miranda* statement from that 1966 case was such a step forward in the protection of a citizen's rights that it was widely hailed as a quantum-leap forward for justice and protection of the innocent. And it was, kinda sorta.

Simultaneously, loud voices screamed that *Miranda* was blanket protection for criminals, who could now get away with almost anything, protected by the wrong arm of the law. Why, we'd never be able to convict anyone anymore! That, of course, turned out to be completely false. Police just had to do their work better, instead of having people convict themselves.

But the ultimate irony and another *non sequitur* in the whole framework of the *Miranda* approach is this: **The people out to convict you are telling you what your rights are**. Is that bass ackwards or what? If you go the next step and make the inane common-wisdom request, "I want *a* lawyer!" you've behaved so foolishly there are no words for it.

You're asking the people collecting the evidence that may put you in the electric chair (and earn themselves a merit badge)—to provide your defense. It might be better than nothing, but what's nothing worth? What you want to say is, "I want to speak to *my* lawyer."

:::

Where does the greatest threat to human freedom come from?

Thomas Jefferson said, "The natural progress of things is for liberty to yield and government to gain ground." Centuries later we can see he was right. *The state* is where the main limits and threats to freedom originate. Your own government presents greater risks to your life, your liberty and your property than criminals or any other source ever could. The Constitution and Bill of Rights were written *expressly* to limit and contain that recognized threat.

After a self-defense shooting, where does the greatest threat to your *individual* freedom come from? Same place. The state.

Who tries to convict you after a shooting? The state.

Who investigates and gathers evidence that can *and will* be used against you in a court of law? The state.

Who runs that court? The state.

Who licenses and regulates the very lawyers you can use in your own defense? The state.

Who advises you to call 911 immediately after you save your life with gunfire? The state.

Who runs the 911 system and its voice recorder? The state.

Who responds to the 911 call? The state.

Who is the main character you should avoid saying *anything* to immediately after you save your life with gunfire? The state.

This is getting pretty repetitious.

Then why do so many experts, including lawyers by the bushel, advise you to immediately call the state after an incident?

This book suggests that calling the state, as the state encourages you to do, may not be the wisest course of action for a person. It's just not in your best interests, and it compromises your freedom and well-established rights. Do you have a right to remain silent or not? Do you have a right to remain silent only after you call the state and have them record your statements?

Do you have a right to an attorney or not? Do you only have a right to an attorney after you call the state and have them record your statements? Is your innocence compromised if you call the state and have them record you without the benefit of an attorney? Yes, it most certainly is.

You're supposed to have a lawyer present during any questioning whatsoever. This book only suggests people should be able to stand on that right, unequivocally, especially after a self-defense shooting, and especially *before* calling 911.

The attorneys I've spoken to pretty much disagree with that. Attorneys, who are after all "officers of the court" and dependent on their state-issued license to operate, pretty much agree that failing to immediately call 911 will go badly for you. Most say they would refuse to make the call even for a good client, and they have their reasons. This seems wrong to me. Their reasons have the same built-in illogic, paradoxes and conflicts of interest you'll find explored throughout this book.

I can see how failure to record yourself on a police recorder immediately after you save your life from a felony assault can be put to the jury to imply you're a heartless insensitive cold-blooded killer, but that seems wrong to me as well. In real terms that means, "You have the right to remain silent but if you do we'll assume you're guilty and we'll use it against you in a court of law and in front of your peers." I say that's bad bad bad and must change.

If you truly faced a jury *of your peers*, that might be different. If the jury-selection process didn't involve questioning called *voir dire* ("to speak the truth," but Latin for "jury rigging" according to many critics of the practice), that might be different. If the jury could be *fully informed*, which the current system does not allow, that might be different. Read about the abuse of the jury system, and the threats a lack of Fully Informed Juries poses to any decent American citizen, at fija.com. It will leave you cold.

I understand that if you fail to get immediate attention for the fallen person, the one who just tried to murder you and failed, it might harm that person's condition. There's no arguing that.

On the other hand though, where does it say you must call 911 immediately and record yourself? Attorney Mitch Vilos, author of *Self Defense Laws of All 50 States*, recalls no state in the union has such a requirement in statute, case law or jury instruction. But he cautions, "Just because there is no affirmative duty in the SD laws, doesn't mean there isn't something lurking in some other obscure part of some lame state's code."

And you do have that niggling right to remain silent, and to have an attorney present, especially at that moment of greatest legal danger to yourself, right after you shoot.

There are only two kinds of 911 call, from a defense attorney's point of view. Terrible ones, and worse ones.

Allow me to point out that, although no states require a 911 call related to self defense, many states do place a statutory duty on people to notify authorities in the event of a hunting accident, and for doctors to report suspicious gunshot wounds.

"However," Vilos notes, as most attorneys do, "my sense is that by not reporting it, it may be alleged as an attempt to cover up or escape. The DA will argue that this is inconsistent with an act of self defense (e.g. 'He had a guilty conscience; that's why he didn't report this shooting'). But you are correct, there are a lot of ways to have authorities notified without dialing 911 yourself and giving a voice recording."

Then he drops the bombshell: "Of all the cases we summarize in *Self Defense Laws of All 50 States,* to illustrate certain principles of SD, it seems in well over half involving a conviction, the defendant's own words to police were critical to the DA's case in obtaining the conviction. (People helped to convict themselves.)

"Giving a statement in hopes of not being arrested could have a lot more serious consequences than going to jail overnight. Even if arrested, your lawyer can always ration out to the DA the reasons you have for using deadly force. And his statements will not be admissible. So you get the same benefit (aside from paying fees), by having your lawyer tell your story to the DA. But your lawyer's statement will be carefully packaged so as not to fry you're butt later."

We should also emphasize that the U.S. Supreme Court has cautioned against implying guilt in a justified use-of-force case, even for a person who leaves the scene and is caught years later. In *Alberty v. U.S.*, 162 U.S. 499 (1896), a lower court had insisted that running away after the fact was a sure sign of guilt. The High Court chastised the judge, saying it is certainly not, "an accepted axiom of criminal law that 'the wicked flee when no man pursueth, but the righteous are as bold as a lion,'" as the lower court judge had instructed the jury.

The High Court rejected that idea emphatically by listing all sorts of reasons why an innocent person might flee after an incident, saying, "[I]t is a matter of common knowledge that men who are entirely innocent do sometimes fly from the scene of a crime through fear of being apprehended as the guilty parties, or from an unwillingness to appear as witnesses... Innocent men sometimes hesitate to confront a jury—not necessarily because they fear that the jury will not protect them, but because they do not wish their names to appear in connection with criminal acts, are humiliated at being obliged to incur the popular odium of an arrest and trial, or because they do not wish to be put to the annoyance or expense of defending themselves."

Granted a new trial, Alberty was acquitted. Today's lawyers would do well to use this forgotten precedent to their clients' advantage.

The Three-Way solution

If your phone has three-way conference calling,
you can get your lawyer on one line, 911 on the other,
and possibly protect yourself from some legal exposures
that way. You call 911 after briefly conferring with your
attorney, but your lawyer does the talking to 911.
It is unclear how this might be treated in court,
since as near as I can tell, it has not been done before.
But it sure sounds like a plan.

CHAPTER SIX
Experts

Massad Ayoob, the prolific author, internationally acclaimed expert in use of lethal force, and former police captain, wrote to me to say:

> Alan, though you've brought many good ideas to the table, this one may not be your best. "Mirandize the police" sounds like someone who planned to show off and tell the cops he knew more about his rights than they did. It does him no good at the same time. For years, I've taught folks to memorize five steps:
>
> 1. "This man attacked me."
>   (Establish from the outset you are the victim complainant, and the guy who got himself shot was the perp.)
> 2. "I will sign the complaint."
>   (Confirmation that you are victim/complainant, and opposite party is perpetrator/suspect.)
> 3. Point out evidence before it disappears.
> 4. Point out witnesses before THEY disappear.
> 5. "Officer, you'll have my full cooperation after I've spoken with counsel."
>
> The Concealed Carry Association has gone with that since, as well. Happy to kick it around with you anytime. Best, Mas.

He has also suggested asking for medical attention for yourself, since you have no way of knowing if you were adversely affected in the confrontation. In fact, if you'll recall, after the attempt on president Reagan's life, he didn't realize he had been shot.

So now that you've read (and maybe liked) my reasoning so far, and the *Adnarim* statement, and maybe thought to yourself, "Well that makes a lot of sense to me," you now have to temper those thoughts with expertise from other quarters. As I said, there is no uniform agreement in this field, plenty of good and bad ideas float around, and of course, "Your results may be different."

The main reasons for talking (besides braggadocio, stupidity and lack of self control) are in hopes of getting off, maintaining good will and avoiding arrest. The main reason for silence is to avoid convicting yourself. These are self-contradictory and mutually exclusive goals.

It's like the classic wisdom in court where the prosecutor makes a case, and the judge says, "You're right." But then the defense makes its case, and the judge says, "You're right." So the bailiff pipes up and says, "But your honor, they can't both be right." And the judge replies dryly, "You're right too."

It's ironic. I like Mas' advice. I think I might take it.

In his 1980 groundbreaking self-defense book, *"In The Gravest Extreme,"* Ayoob goes down this familiar path:

> Let us suppose that the unlikely events considered here have come to pass: you have been compelled to kill in defense of yourself, your family, or other innocent persons. *Your first act should be to call an ambulance; your second, to call the police* (emphasis added).

> Expect to be arrested and charged with murder. Most statutes stipulate clearly that the perpetrator of any homicide be charged with murder, unless the evidence of the prosecution (i.e., the decision of the police investigators) obviously indicates

that the killing was justified.

Explain to the arresting officers that you're not a punk taking the Fifth, but you'd rather wait until you spoke with your attorney before making an official statement. Call your attorney *as soon as you've notified the police and emergency units* (my emphasis again).

MAKE NO STATEMENTS WHATEVER TO THE PRESS. Newsmen have found that murder sells more papers than justifiable homicide, and shooting incidents tend to become distorted by the time they reach the printed page. You may think that you'll be treated like a hero for killing a criminal. You're probably wrong.

He goes on to describe a front-page headline "news" item that reads like: "Crazy old guy shoots youngster for making noise." The truth came out weeks later in a small blurb in the back of the paper: "Elderly gentleman shoots gang banger after thug breaks into living room." The rest of *In The Gravest Extreme* just keeps getting better. It is outstanding.

So let's look at what the U.S. Supreme Court said, since they're the genesis of the government officer's *Miranda* statement to you the citizen. For an interrogation to be admissible in court:

"...the person in custody must, prior to interrogation, be clearly informed that he or she has the right to remain silent, and that anything the person says will be used against that person in court; the person must be clearly informed that he or she has the right to consult with an attorney and to have that attorney present during questioning, and that, if he or she indigent, an attorney will be provided at no cost to represent her or him." (*Miranda v. Arizona*, 384 U.S. 436, 1966, 81 words)

This has been turned into various statements in different parts of the country, and subsequent court decisions have suggested that the suspect must understand what's going on, so yes-or-no questions have been inserted to make an interrogation more airtight. For example, this thorough version:

YOUR MIRANDA RIGHTS

You have the right to remain silent and refuse to answer questions. Do you understand? Anything you do say can and will be used against you in a court of law. Do you understand? You have the right to consult an attorney before speaking to the police and to have an attorney present during questioning now or in the future. Do you understand? If you cannot afford an attorney, one will be appointed for you before any questioning if you wish. Do you understand? If you decide to answer questions now without an attorney present you will still have the right to stop answering at any time until you talk to an attorney. Do you understand? Knowing and understanding your rights as I have explained them to you, are you willing to answer my questions without an attorney present? (139 words)

So there are the rights you get as the police "Mirandize" you. One attorney actually suggested saying, "No," every time you're asked if you understand. This could help in court, he says, and face it, you do not understand. What does it actually mean for them to appoint an attorney—how soon, who is the person, can you switch, will it cost anything, can you have two to confer with each other, can you additionally bring in your own, do you have to get arrested first? Of course you don't understand.

The ACLU, in their widely circulated "Bust Card," goes far afield and makes many recommendations:

- Think carefully about your words, movement, body language, and emotions.
- Don't get into an argument with the police.
- Remember, anything you say or do can be used against you.
- Keep your hands where the police can see them.
- Don't run. Don't touch any police officer.
- Don't resist even if you believe you are innocent.
- Don't complain on the scene or tell the police they're wrong or that you're going to file a complaint.
- Do not make any statements regarding the incident.

- Ask for a lawyer immediately upon your arrest.
- Remember officers' badge & patrol car numbers.
- Write down everything you remember ASAP.
- Try to find witnesses and their names and phone numbers.
- If you are injured, take photographs of the injuries as soon as possible, but make sure you seek medical attention first.
- If you feel your rights have been violated, file a written complaint with police department's internal affairs division or civilian board, or call the ACLU hotline, 1-877-634-5454.

Think carefully about your *emotions* they say. Is that a contradiction in terms or what? How do you follow that instruction? Although many of these ideas seem to have merit, acting upon them goes right back to the problem of calling 911 before your support team knows you're making the call.

An organization called Border Angels recommends use of a statement on a card if confronted by law enforcement. Unlike the proposed *Adnarim* statement, which is intended to keep an innocent person out of trouble, Border Angels is trying to prevent illegal aliens from being detected and dealt with legally. Their website is borderangels.org/knowyourrights.html. Their carry card, which they recommend handing to immigration officials or the police, says:

> Please be informed that I am choosing to exercise my right to remain silent and the right to refuse to answer your questions. If I am detained, I request to contact my attorney immediately. I am also exercising my right to refuse to sign anything until I consult with my attorney. Thank you.

Ken Hanson, author of *The Ohio Guide to Firearm Laws*, has his own view of the subject. In response to my request for comment on the *Adnarim* statement, he replied:

> I've never seen too much utility to this approach in criminal cases (i.e., prepared remarks) versus just stating at the first

contact, "I wish to consult with my attorney." There are no rights to invoke; you have the rights all the time, you must knowingly, intelligently and voluntarily waive them through affirmative action. [Note: a new Supreme Court case now requires you to clearly invoke.] A card with wording like the one proposed is honestly more likely to terminate any good will chances you would have during the encounter. Every police encounter is a negotiation from the beginning up until the point that the good will is burned up. Saying things like "do not attempt to violate my rights" and get me "a glass of water" and you might as well waive a red flag in front of their face.

I disagree with the attorney who said the card would be used at jury trial. The only time it would be used is if you choose to use it. Invoking a right is not admissible evidence against the defendant. As a prosecutor, I can't even ask an officer if he read someone their rights and then they refused to give a statement. I really am not able to even comment on the lack of a statement. A different approach would be:

"I do not waive, explicitly or by implication, any of my rights and do not consent to undertake any action that is voluntary on my part. I will follow all of your lawful directions to the extent these directions do not require my consent or waiver of any rights, and my compliance with a lawful order does not constitute my consent to that action nor waiver of any right. I require immediate consultation with my attorney before proceeding any further."

Ken's advice has a serious ring of experience to it. His proposed statement is authoritative yet it goes against some other comments that have suggested simple plain English so even a regular police officer could understand it. We're not the Supreme Court, so none of these suggestions are going to have their gravitas. I personally believe a balance between legalese and dumb-down English may be the best choice.

The issue of good will is a crucial one but an ambiguous one. Sure, if the police are on your side from the get go that's a good thing. If you tick them off that won't help. Does that have any legal play? Very little. Could it shift the direction of subsequent activity? Absolutely. In your favor? Possibly. Will reading an *Adnarim* statement cast you as an innocent or as a smart ass, with predictable results?

If you are perceived by the police as the good guy, innocent of any wrongdoing in a perfectly clean shoot, word quickly goes up and down the line that this is a no-bill, and your road is smoothly paved. If you burn up any good will you might otherwise have, every step you take will be hindered and encumbered. Can you do anything to reliably control that ambiance? Mebbe. Simply remaining mute can sway that for or against you.

Attorney Sean Healy in Texas is rightfully nervous about the whole thing:

> Frankly this scares me because it could be construed as giving legal advice.
>
> I would advise you to discuss this with several criminal defense attorneys. Have them compare their advice for a self-defense incident to a DWI stop. I've heard from a number of attorneys and other experts, and they all give different advice. In the self-defense context, my own personal opinion is 1) Be sure you call 911 first, so they write your name after "Victim" and the other party's name after "Suspect." 2) If you had to use force, give them the basics (I was afraid he was going to kill me; I didn't have a choice; I defended myself) then find a reason to stop talking.
>
> One thing is clear—in that situation a person's perceptions and verbal skills will be degraded by adrenaline and a lot of other factors. Talking in too much detail could cause mistakes that "can and will be used against you." Plus your lawyer needs to know everything you tell them. You might, if truthful, say your chest hurts and ask for a doctor. You might say you welcome the chance to talk with them in more detail, but you want to talk to your lawyer first. I don't think there is one answer that works for all situations and jurisdictions.

Sean agrees with and independently adopts many of the principles Ayoob believes are best, but then goes on to negate advice that's widely suggested, by making four declarative statements that can *and will* come back to haunt him: "I was afraid; He was going to kill me; I didn't have a choice; I defended myself."

In the hands of a great prosecutor out to nail you, those will transmogrify into: I became irrational, I can determine intent and predict the future, I neglected all choices but deadly force; I committed the homicide you see here (or maybe just, I shot and killed the dead human being you see covered in blood over there).

Attorney Mark Moritz, a very knowledgeable firearms enthusiast and local friend whose field of practice is not criminal law, made some of the most telling observations I received:

> I think the whole point of the card is to eliminate the need to remember even five words; just hold up a card. (I do agree the sentences should be short, though. Compare the *Miranda* warning—short, direct sentences, carefully designed to be understandable by an illiterate ditch-digger. "You have the right to remain silent." Bam, a seven-word sentence. We should do likewise.)

> The bigger problem is the overwhelming compulsion to talk, talk, talk, talk, and talk some more. People who have shot other people report that they are just bursting to talk, and the real challenge is to exercise the self-control to Speak The Fewest Utterances. [Note the acronym for Mark's suggestion has a colloquial corollary.]

> As to five popular specific words, which I have heard for many years, I have not been persuaded. Confessing to "fear" gives a hostile prosecutor an opening, some rope to hang you. A person under the influence of fear is terrified, irrational, unable to think clearly, or act the way a "reasonable man" would. No need to go there. You can tell the jury that, if you get that far, but it is irrelevant to a police contact.

"I feared for my life" is also an implied confession that you shot the bad guy: "I feared for my life; that's why I shot him." That's something the prosecution needs to prove. Let them do their job; I ain't confessing.

I learned that back in 1982, when Phoenix police officers "Big John" Davis and "Nacho" Conchos got into an arm's-length gunfight with a bank robber in a dark bar. They both emptied their revolvers at the guy; he shot them with a .32. They both died of their wounds, but lived long enough to swear that they had shot the bank robber—and there he was, dead on the bar room floor. However, forensic examination showed that Davis and Conchos had missed with all of their shots, and the bank robber died of a .32 in the head. He had killed himself, but in the excitement neither Davis nor Conchos nor any of the witnesses had seen that.

If I "fear for my life," and empty my gun at the bad guy at close range, and he falls down, *probably* I shot him. But I don't know that for a fact. He may have shot himself. He may have been shot by another person that I didn't notice, who slipped out the back door. He may have had a heart attack. He may have died of a drug overdose. He may have been struck by lightning. I'll wait for the ballistics report and the surveillance videotape before I admit that I shot anybody.

"I feared for my life" also does not cut off questioning. "You feared for your life? Why? Is that why you shot him? Tell me more about that." *Miranda*-warning case law says that the warning must be unambiguous (e.g., *Doody v. Schriro*, a mass-murderer case) and any waiver of rights must also be unambiguous. An assertion of rights should be unambiguous, too (e.g., *U.S. v. Jose Rodriguez*). Talking about your fears does not equal an assertion of rights. "No statements. No questions. No searches. Want lawyer." Those are the things you need to say. Those are the only things you should say. Alan is just looking for a good way to phrase it.

Mark continues his clear thinking:

This card is supposed to be for general use, not specifically for gunfights. Could be your neighbor is pissed off about your dog pooping on his lawn, so called the cops to report you are operating a meth lab. Could be a report that your yard guy is an illegal alien. Could be all kinds of things not involving shooting. Whether you have been Mirandized or not, detained or not, arrested or not, you always have the rights to silence, lawyer, and freedom from searches.

Back when I was writing for the gun magazines (with a quill, on parchment), I had occasion to interview a fellow who owned a biker bar, and who had gotten into a shootout with about seven bikers. IIRC, he killed a couple, and wounded a couple, but took a couple of serious life-threatening torso hits from a .357 and a .41. He told me that as the ER docs were prepping him for surgery, two cops came in and started to ask him questions! He refused to answer questions, and one of the cops gave him the line about, "Well, I guess you must have something to hide." He told them something along the lines of "Maybe you can get away with that stuff with teenagers, but I know better than to answer questions. Get lost."

Thus I have no illusions about police officers acting sympathetically to somebody who claims to feel sick or have chest pains (as Ayoob has hinted), much less somebody who feels a little thirsty. Hell, they don't give a rat's ass if you have a couple of bullet holes in you, and a nurse is shoving a tube up your pee pee. You'll be damn lucky if they don't hit you with the Taser, pepper spray you right there on the gurney, and then charge you with resisting arrest and assaulting a police officer.

However, I have been thinking about the water question, and I think I may have something even better! "Officer, I need to go to the bathroom. Where can I go?" Now, if the cop says "Just go in your pants," then do it. I think a jury would be really pissed off (so to speak) if a police officer refused permission to go find a bathroom to take a leak, for God's sake.

And never ever forget, anything you say can and will be used against you. The operant word is *anything*. I shot this guy. I didn't shoot this guy. I don't know who this guy is. I had nothing to do with this. Any phrase or statement can and will be used against you. I'm a lawyer, trust me, anything can be bent to mean whatever a lawyer wants it to mean. Speak The Fewest Utterances.

Even saying "I want to talk to my lawyer," can be used against you! While it should stop the police right then and there, everyone knows it may not. A hostile police officer can use that to say "Then you must have something to hide," and encourage you to disprove him, squeezing out statements you should not make.

You can see why I like this guy. He makes a good argument for using the simplest English and avoiding legalistic sounding terms:

> Whatever is on this card is likely to be presented to a jury, projected on a large screen. It needs to sound like the jurors talk. Jurors need to be able to identify with it, sympathetically. "Whatsoever" is a high-falutin' word that we rarely use in normal conversation: "I don't want any ketchup on my fries, whatsoever." "I respectfully insist"? Sheesh. The statement needs to be self-serving; it should make you look like The Good Guy. Re-think this whole card thing, and write it so that a juror thinks, "That's exactly what I would have said, and how I would have said it." Maybe 1) something short and sweet, or 2) an adjustment to *Miranda* itself:

> 1. "Please don't ask me any questions. I have been advised never to answer any questions or make any statements until I have met with my attorney. I do not consent to any searches. Thank you for your understanding."

> 2. "I invoke my right to remain silent. Because anything I say can and will be used against me in a court of law, I will not say anything. I invoke my right to an attorney, and I want to have an attorney present during questioning."

> It also seems to me that I am not interested in cooperating. Cooperating in what? Cooperating in putting me in jail? No thanks. Cooperating in discovering "the truth"? A) That's not my job, and B) that's not necessarily how the police and the prosecutor view their jobs, either. That statement is not necessary or helpful. "I refuse to consent" and "I do not consent" achieve the same result, but the former sounds belligerent.

Not all the experts gave expert advice. Lawyers like to give advice, and never forget that some will opine regardless of any ability to do so intelligently. This one's a nice guy, and he took up my invitation to comment, but should have taken the common advice to say nothing. At least it's a good example:

> Good morning/afternoon/evening officer. Let me first say that I understand that you have a difficult, dangerous, and often thankless job. I am thankful to you and to officers like you who

risk their lives every day to uphold law and order in our civil
society. I recognize that your goal is to return safe to your loved
ones. I would be happy to reasonably cooperate with you on
matters of officer safety. However, my respect for you must be
matched by your respect for me and my constitutional rights,
which both of us believe are the foundation of our legal system.
[He then quotes a portion of the *Adnarim* statements and
concludes:] Although I will remain silent after reading this
statement to you, I will close by saying that I am pleased to
meet you and can only wish we met under different
circumstances.

I can't actually say I disagree with most of what he says,
but I surely wouldn't say it that way, or at all. You want
to get off, not get empathy.

Attorney Marc Victor, who is an Arizona-based Certified
Specialist in Criminal Law says keep it short and sweet:

Alan, I'm happy to help. However, after a self-defense incident,
or more accurately stated, an incident that the shooter believes
and hopes is a self-defense incident, what to say is, "I want to
talk to my lawyer now." I have difficulty thinking of much more
to say. Your thoughts?

Marc also offers a prepared statement on the back of his
business card for all the years I have know him:

I refuse to consent to any search whatsoever. As such, I do not
consent to a search of my premises, my person, my immediate
location or any vehicle or effects. I hereby exercise my rights as
enumerated by the Fourth, Fifth, Sixth, Ninth and Fourteenth
Amendments to the United States Constitution and Article Two
of the Arizona Constitution. **I demand to have my attorney
present prior to and throughout any questioning at all.**
Additionally, I wish to consult with my attorney prior to any
discussion with law enforcement officers on the subject of
waiver.

A law professor at a prestigious university comments:

Very interesting! Looks sound to me. But I'm not sure that a
blanket statement "I am interested in cooperating" is generally
accurate, or particularly helpful.

Prolific author, historian, firearms expert and friend Barrett Tillman makes a few salient observations:

> In my decidedly non-legal opinion, the *Adnarim* statement is excellent and says everything that needs saying—except maybe "Tell me, officer, is it true that you have 72 hours to give a statement after a shooting, with the Fraternal Order of Police lawyer present?" The concern that a prosecutor will twist it is likely real: "So, Mr. Gunowner, you had this thing all printed up ready to justify your heinous actions on the day you were just waiting for!?" Whether a Jury of Our Peers would interpret such a document as evidence of Heinous Intentions is of course a toss-up. But if it's on the back of your lawyer's card, that seems proof that it is not ginned up by you, nor intended solely for Your Heinous Purpose.

An attorney at a well-known gun-rights lobbying group whose job means he must remain anonymous says:

> You can't bind an officer with any words other than "I demand my attorney be present before I speak." This alone will lead to a LOT of rough treatment that will never be looked into. And prior to Mirandizing you the cops will just talk to each other, in front of you, swapping stories designed to make you wet yourself for fear. Making the statement before you produce identification could get you charged with resisting arrest and certainly get you labeled as "uncooperative."

The "uncooperative" issue comes up again and again. You don't want to burn up any good will you may have. Once it's used up you can never get it back. Acting like a real smart ass and asking, "What is your reasonably articulable suspicion officer?" as one prolific gun author suggests, "is just the sort of attitude that will get you Tasered, and charged with 'resisting arrest' when you hit the officer in the knee with your groin," according to Moritz. One expert says police will recognize the card routine in about two seconds. So, that's a deterrent to exercising your rights? You recognize the *Miranda* routine in under two seconds, does that make it wrong?

Another says, "I like the suggestion of a 'cooling off' period before a debrief—an established protocol to let the adrenaline wear off. Unfortunately, adrenaline is partly responsible for the running of the mouth, and, it happens to everyone. Maybe the card should include, "Rule #1 - Adrenaline is making me stupid and say things before my attorney gets here and tells me to shut-up. I must fight the adrenaline and make as few utterances as necessary, which is almost nothing (name rank & serial number)." Rule #2 - re-read rule #1 again, and again, and again, until the lawyer arrives.

Bob Irwin, owner of The Gun Store in Las Vegas and author of three books, has personally trained 14,000 people. He's interviewed about 90 who have actually shot another person. About 80 of the shooters are security guards or LEOs of some sort, and by the way, in most cases the person shot survived.

In all but about five instances, the shooters "blather on the 911 call and fail to heed any of the common advice to just say ambulance needed and stop talking." The five who controlled themselves were "highly trained and experienced operatives." Police friends of his tell him they don't like the advice of "don't talk to the police." However, if a friend were to call and ask them personally for advice, they'd of course say don't talk, another fundamental paradox in this mess.

Attorney Richard Stevens, who represents federal law enforcement agents, raises flags over "interested in cooperating" (the meaning is unclear); "this instruction" (that's contentious); "without any purpose of evasion" (unclear again); "insist" ("ask" is less confrontational) and he says:

The card wouldn't be perfect, of course. But consider that even if the victim-citizen were too tongue-tied to recite the whole thing, then she could just give it to the cops, or recite part.

Now, if she had made others aware she had the card—and/or if there were witnesses on scene, then she'd be able to testify at the preliminary hearing that she had the card, and that she read the card to them and/or gave it to them. If even her possessing the card could be corroborated, then the police would be in a bind trying to deny her testimony.

Sometimes litigation is not about you proving something is true. Sometimes it is about making the other guy disprove what you have shown is likely or plausible.

As an aside, the challenge in defense of an agent can be to cooperate with authorities but not hand them a criminal case against the client. I need to balance between his possibly poor choice of words—at the same time that the authorities need to know what happened so they could close the file.

A highly regarded state Superior Court judge notes that:

I like your reverse *Miranda* statement, but I would not worry about it being shown or read to a jury. A judge would be very unlikely to allow that to happen. It would be tantamount to admitting evidence of the Defendant's refusal to incriminate himself or his demand to see an attorney. Those matters are generally not discussed in front of the jury. If they are germane to a legal ruling made necessary by a motion lodged by either the prosecution or the defense, they are addressed outside the presence of the jury, usually during a pretrial hearing.

An attorney in Tucson, who practices in another field but enjoys firearms enough to have arranged to visit the SHOT Show on her own dime, had insightful comments:

Probably the more critical thing to think about is how reaching for a card and reading it to the police after a shooting will come across to a jury. Juries think about how they would respond to such an event and judge the defendant's actions accordingly. It might come across to them as contrived (and a prosecutor might argue, evidence of premeditation) for a person (especially anyone who might be painted as a gun enthusiast, aka "nut") to carry around a card to read to the police in the event they are involved in a shooting.

Also, if you shoot the intruder and do not immediately call 911 thereafter, but instead call your lawyer and have your lawyer call the police, your actions will likely seem suspect to a typical juror. I remember discussing the idea of asking for a glass of water with you back in December at the gun show. That's not a bad idea because it seems like something a reasonable person would do in the moment and would necessarily give you a moment to gather your thoughts and calm down. Also, as you then pointed out, it might be likely to encourage the police to view you as a victim needing their aid rather than a suspected criminal.

The bottom line is that often the best answer a lawyer can give you is, "It depends." From my experience, there are few cases where a "one size fits all" approach works without a hitch.

Phoenix attorney Steve Twist likes the idea of being armed with information, and thinks the *Adnarim* idea is OK as far as its words go. Sure, be informed ahead of time, have a plan and plan to stay calm. But like the majority of lawyers, he doesn't go for the suggestion to call your lawyer first, because of the implication of guilt.

I'm concerned about what the jury might think. First thing, call for emergency services. I'm very sympathetic to the problem you describe, Alan, but calling your attorney could hurt the gun owner. Call to report that there's been a shooting and to get someone to the scene right away. Maybe what's needed is a jury instruction to protect the person who makes the call. Find out how much psychological research and evidence there is to support the idea that statements made in that situation are unreliable and should be discounted.

Keith Manning, the deputy Maricopa County attorney, in a public presentation, pointed out that the first person to call 911 is seen as the victim, and suggests that a person with a guilty conscience won't call. When you call 911, he says identify yourself and your address, describe yourself so you won't get shot by accident, and say "There's been a shooting, send police and an ambulance," and put the phone down.

Don't alter the scene, and protect the bad guy's weapon (one other expert cautioned not to get your fingerprints on it). Expect to have guns pointed at you—you'll be a suspect and are a potential threat. Agree to testify against the perp, and to cooperate later after you speak with counsel. He pointed out that his police officers have an attorney on call 24/7. Two, actually.

Author and speaker Marc MacYoung has written extensively on the topic of when to shoot, how to avoid an incident, and self defense. One of his greatest concerns addresses the mindset of officials you'll face:

People *must* understand when it is time to pull the trigger and *when it is not*. It's not about feelings, fear, emotions or perceptions—it must be based on articulable facts—that the shooter must be able to identify and explain.

What people don't understand is that most DA's (or at least all of them that I have met) have a biased perspective. It can be summed up as "everything is a crime—especially if someone dies." This is terrifying.

Cops, DAs and attorneys hear the SD claim all the time. After SODDI (some other dude did it) fails, claiming 'self defense' is what an aggressor/combatant/criminal does—you can damn near set your watch by it. This is why I say *the self-defense pool has been peed in*. The problem with a self-defense claim is that in 90% of the cases *it wasn't*. Odds are it was a consensual fight or an outright assault. It's someone trying to avoid punishment.

The bias I'm talking about is that when they hear 'self-defense,' DAs and cops automatically assume you're lying. They've forgotten, or have chosen to ignore, that the 10% *still* exists.

So the cops/DA's questions are slanted and biased in order to trip people up into confessing that *it wasn't self-defense*. This is a key point to know—especially when it *was* self-defense. It's about keeping your mouth shut until your attorney arrives. Exercise your *Miranda* rights—and you *must* state this to the investigating officers (the Supreme Court just ruled on that point). Keep your mouth shut—and this includes sitting in the jail cell. Jailhouse snitches are looking for ways to lighten their sentences by cooperating with prosecutors.

Prosecution's lack of understanding what actual self-defense is—blended with this assumption of guilt—leads me to say something that is not technically accurate, but is a critical for gun owners to understand: *"If you claim self-defense, assume the burden of proof has shifted onto you."*

Let me again stress that is not technically accurate, but is a functional rule of thumb. Officially the burden of proof is on the state. Defense attorneys usual strategy is to undermine the state's evidence and create "reasonable doubt." Putting that into plain English, that means the state says "This is the evidence, this is why we believe he did this crime." The defense attorney goes "Is not! Liar liar, pants on fire! Neener! Neener!" Obviously this is a gross over-simplification, but it gets an important idea across. If the jury isn't convinced by the state's evidence, the person is not convicted.

If you used your gun in self-defense, you'd better be ready to bring a preponderance of evidence that cannot be dismissed, minimized or twisted around by the DA. That's why I'm such a big fan of training—not about shooting—but *when* to shoot and equally important when to *stop* shooting. I'm also a big advocate of joining the Armed Citizen's Legal Defense Network and the Second Amendment Foundation, *before* you start carrying. You'll need their kind of information to help justify your actions to a legal system that assumes you're lying about self-defense. And while we're on the subject, such groups can help you find lawyers who know how to defend an innocent person. *Most attorney's don't know what real self-defense is* and they'll try to defend you like you're guilty. This will get you convicted if you were acting in self-defense.

Carrying a gun is a big responsibility. Using it, well, let's just say the bad repercussions mean you'd better be in immediate danger of death or grave bodily injury. The results of pulling the trigger will be terrible. The only thing that will make that worth it is if the results of not pulling the trigger will be worse.

I always tell people that if they are going to carry a gun they must conduct themselves to a higher standard because they will be held to one. Their actions have repercussions and they can't just lip off. Basically the rule is: "Gun or bad attitude, one gets left at home."

A corporate attorney who is also active in gun-rights issues on the East Coast made a very rare but welcomed admission of a lack of proper experience to comment meaningfully:

> I like the idea of the *Adnarim* statement generally, very much. I haven't commented because I don't practice criminal law (only civil - commercial), so I don't have the needed expertise to provide meaningful or insightful comment. Other than that I like the idea generally. A lot.

Gun-law author and attorney Kevin Jamison makes some of the classic contradictory remarks ("Say this, and remain silent") but closes with a salient thought:

> Call 911 yourself. If you call a lawyer you will be accused of cooking up a story. Say: 1. He tried to kill me! 2. I was never so scared in my life! 3. Send an ambulance. There is some case law in Missouri that if you don't proclaim your innocence at the earliest possible opportunity, the prosecutor gets to mention that in court. You *must* say you were afraid in the 911 call.
>
> When the police arrive they will want more. Remember SHIELD—Silence, He attacked me (I am the victim), I am Innocent (some law on this), there is the Evidence, I want a Lawyer. I heard of a man who defended himself and he was sued (Bernard Goetz and others) I'm afraid of being sued and I want a lawyer (cops get sued all the time). Don't resist, it looks bad, and they will just bring enough cops to make it happen. Don't consent to questioning, searches, tests, statements, anything until your lawyer gets there. There is no perfect solution for an imperfect situation.

In an article he published on the subject Jamison makes some very illuminating comments, reproduced here with his permission:

> In a death penalty case, the Missouri Supreme Court found that the defendant had purchased a used car which sported the bumper sticker, *"I'm the person your mother warned you about."* At trial the prosecution argued that the fact he did not remove this bumper sticker revealed something about his character. The Missouri Supreme Court ruled that it was perfectly acceptable for the state to kill this man, in part, because of his

failure to remove the bumper sticker. Imagine the effect of bumper stickers bought in jest such as, *"Keep Honking, I'm Reloading."* If this case does not inspire a re-evaluation of one's T-shirt collection, nothing will...

There is a cynical defense attorney saying: *"Anything you say will be misquoted and used against you."* In the movie "My Cousin Vinnie," two unfortunate Yankees are suspected of murder and during questioning are accused of shooting a clerk. One incredulously asked, *"I shot the clerk?"* This is taken down and read in court as a confession. Theater audiences laughed, defense attorneys smiled and nodded. There have even been cases where comments by other persons have been attributed to the defendant, and used against him; complete silence is the only bulwark against these mistakes...

But here again we have those contradictory directives to remain absolutely silent, and to speak into the police recorder or make other statements:

The first statement is the 911 call. These calls are recorded and if the call sounds bad for the defendant, it will be played over and over again at trial...

The demand for a lawyer is both the best thing one can do, and a damaging statement. Anyone who is questioned by police has the right to a lawyer; this includes victims. The problem is that the police, and potential jurors, take a demand for a lawyer as evidence of something to hide. To compound the problem, the victim's decision to remain silent and demand for a lawyer can be used again the victim in court. In the criminal system, one does not have rights, until arrested; it doesn't have to make sense, it's just the law [Note: there isn't universal agreement on that]. It is a left-handed fortune that people who act in self-defense are routinely arrested. It may be called something else such as "detained" or the Alice-in-Wonderland explanation "You're being handcuffed for your own protection." Whenever a person is not allowed to leave, the person is placed under arrest regardless of descriptive terms...

Self-defense cases bring out the curious, the media in the forefront. Comments to friends will be confused and used against you, comments to family will be mistaken and used against you. Both family and friends can be subpoenaed and forced to testify against you. Comments to the media will be sensationalized and this is never good. The New York City prosecutor's office had determined not to charge Bernard Goetz, until he made unwise remarks to the news media. At some point a statement must be made. The impression is that the earlier a statement is made, the more reliable it is. In reality, the earlier a statement is made, the less reliable it is. The effects of stress will confuse the statement and even cause temporary amnesia. Inaccuracies in the initial statement will convince authorities that the survivor is both a liar and a murderer. A lawyer must be immediately engaged to organize the statement...

A lawyer is a professional storyteller. He will not tell the client how to lie, he will tell him how to tell the truth, a more complicated process than most imagine. The statement must contain facts that track the elements of self-defense.

Second Amendment scholar, author, videographer and attorney Dave Hardy had this to say:

If the officer reads the *Miranda* warnings, I'd suggest just shutting up and saying you want to talk to an attorney first. That ends it. If you can reach an attorney, they will tell you to shut up. Reason: *Miranda* warnings only have to be read if the person is in custody. There's nothing that forbids them being read earlier, but in practice, by the time the officer reads them, he has made the decision to arrest, and there is no sense trying to talk him out of it. Just shut up. As to the rest, refuse when asked to consent to search.

But there is no sense volunteering that you refuse before the officer has asked. He probably won't, and volunteering just gets the officer curious—sort of like "you aren't going to ask to see what's in my trunk, are you?" My experience with Tucson cops, anyway, is that they are pro-gun. No sense making them wonder. Handed one the .45 from my glove compartment, he asked if I had a CCW permit, I said no, and he started encouraging me to get one.

Evan Nappen, a lawyer deeply involved in heavy-duty firearm litigation takes the remain-silent approach and points out, as few lawyers did, that once you fail to remain silent, your refusal to gab can possibly be brought up in trial:

Alan, It's a fun idea, but this will most likely be used against the defendant by the State. This is a statement, when in fact the "suspect" should not be making any statements. The fact that a person remains silent cannot normally be mentioned or used against a person at trial. This "Reverse *Miranda*" could be used by the State to undermine the Fifth Amendment and get the defendant's unwillingness to talk brought before the jury who will surely think "If he had nothing to hide why didn't he talk." Remaining silent means just that. Just ask for your lawyer and shut up.

A prominent attorney for a major gun-rights lobbying organization emphasizes the effect any statement and your actions can have on the police at the scene:

It might well be considered unfairly prejudicial to use the defendant's invocation of the Fifth Amendment against him.

I would be less concerned about the effect on a citizen's legal rights in court, than on the effect reading a statement like this would have on the dynamic with the investigating officer. I'd be very interested to hear what any police officers might tell you about the proposed language. An investigating officer who finds the good guy standing over the body of a deceased armed robber with a phone in his hand and his gun on the ground may initially think he has a simple self-defense case, but if the citizen then whips out a card and reads a script like this, the officer may well reconsider and wonder if the good guy is a little too prepared.

The scripted request for a glass of water would only add to this, in my view, as would preemptively answering questions that haven't been asked yet. A simple statement (not read from a card) along the lines of "Nothing like this has happened to me before... I'll be happy to cooperate with you, but I really think I should talk to a lawyer first" (repeat as needed) would effectively invoke the person's rights but not raise the officer's eyebrows.

Tim Forshey is an attorney who handles the law portion of CCW training for one of the premier gun clubs in Arizona, the Scottsdale Gun Club. He says:

I like it, a lot, and I "get" the glass of water reference. It worries me on two counts:

1) A lot of the people I've been involved with helping were in

such an emotional state following the event that they probably couldn't have handled even something this simplistic and "recipe-like" under the stress following a shooting or other threatened use of lethal force, and,

2) You and I know that there are a fair number of cops who will view this as uncooperative and "sassy" and who will react just the opposite of how we'd like them to act.

As far as being "required" to call 911—I'm aware of no statutory directive to do so, but I believe you are required to report a shooting (don't have any cite handy, but I'm pretty sure there is one). [Note: Arizona has a report-required statute for hunting accidents and for doctors treating suspicious wounds, but not for citizen self-defense incidents.] But, if you don't call, you're probably exposing yourself to additional problems, such as the allegation or conclusion that your failure to summon help in the quickest possible manner led to additional pain, suffering, injuries or death on the part of the person shot.

I have used a quick call to 911 in more than one case, two of which were jury trials, to show that the defendant had nothing to hide, and to point out that calling is not what a true "bad guy" does after committing a crime. In at least one of those trials, at least one juror positively agreed and said it helped her reach a not guilty vote. The recording of the call can, of course, be troubling, but it can also be a big positive factor in the choice not to indict. The statement certainly could be offered as evidence, subject to a judge's discretion as to prejudicial effect, and it could probably be argued to cut either way in a jury's determination. Interesting concept, for sure!

The notion that a would-be murderer who failed deserves immediate life-saving attention is distressing to say the least. But it's easy to see how this could sway a gullible or poorly informed jury in the murderer's favor by a crafty silken-tongued prosecutor.

However, the fact that the only perpetrator you can see is down does not mean you're out of the woods yet, and it remains perfectly reasonable to first guarantee your own safety and the safety of other innocents, before turning attention to the neutralized would-be killer. Since you do face possible execution, long-term imprisonment or civil liability for the shots fired, ignoring your own legal safety is not wholly unreasonable, despite how the system might use that against you. The attacker showed zero regard for your safety. You must show plenty. How fair is that?

The advice of too many trainers I reached fell right into the self-contradictory, or say-only-this, or impossible-to-follow categories. Guys who thoroughly enjoy guns and know how to shoot can be pretty deficient in legal areas, but that doesn't stop them from spreading their opinions as if they were words from the Supreme Court. This trainer was different. Bill Davison has extensive combat experience on several continents and runs the Tac Pro Shooting Center on hundreds of acres in Texas where he trains tactical military and police units as well as the general public.

We don't have a hand out on this but we talk about it in class. Key points are: Firstly, understand that all non-normal bodily functions (i.e. defecating or urinating on yourself under stress) should be addressed immediately by requesting medical attention. Treat any dizziness, faintness or chest pain the same way.

All of these reactions indicate the immensely heightened stress level of someone in fear of their life. Although these things may not happen to a well-trained individual, they often occur in a deadly-force situation. Any 12 reasonable people would immediately understand that you literally have the crap scared out of you if you were in fear of your life.

We understand that due to the adrenaline dump and blood being pulled to the central organs of the body, the eyes end up with tunnel vision and the ears have auditory exclusion. (The first time one shoots a deer they usually have no hearing protection on but do not suffer the usual "oh shit that was loud" that is seen with negligent discharge or firing a weapon on the range with no hearing protection on.) We also know that during this time, the brain files all the information of the situation and it can take up to 12 to 24 hours to remember the whole incident.

With all these things in mind, we then remind students that when dispatched to a shooting, the police officer also is in a heightened state of cautiousness. It is up to the student to understand that until the situation is explained, he is just another person with a gun, who the police officer must confront. So you should, as soon as the situation is under control, re-holster or put the gun on the ground and put both hands up, and verbalize with the officer explaining that you are the good guy and the bad is "over there."

You should be polite and courteous, give a brief outline of the threat, and then ask for your attorney. During the delay in the attorney's appearance, you should not talk about the incident. Although this can aggravate the officer in charge, it is a fact that all the facts will not come out until your brain has had time to process them. At that time, you would relay the whole situation to your attorney and then with your attorney to the police.

You must understand and relay to the police officer that you are the victim here and defending yourself is a scary and stressful situation that no one would wish on themselves, and you just wanted to do the right thing.

:::

So—did you notice the one thing missing in the advice of all these experts? Not one said, "In a case where a person used a prepared statement when the police arrived, this is what happened in court." Not one. All we have here—and they all are bona fide experts in their fields—is opinion, supposition, well-educated conjecture and synthesized wisdom. There may be a case of someone using a "get-out-of-jail-card"—or a "go-directly-to-jail-card" depending on who's naming it—but I couldn't find one. Experts overlooked that in their remarks.

That's because, I suspect, all of these are examples of **"cold air"** (the opposite of hot air). Gun-rights types—myself included—just love to expound on the what-ifs of gunfighting. A lack of hard information is no deterrent to the conversations that go on endlessly, or show up when authors author, bloggers blog or writers write.

"Cold air" is the tendency to speak about what you think is real, and really get off on it, without any shred of cold cold reality involved. That's not to say cold air doesn't have value, or that there aren't examples out there of evidence-based card-carrying gunfighting policy, but it's scarce—and it's important to recognize when the much more common cold air is blowing in your face. Cold air blows over caliber and stopping power, tactical response, sights, barrel length, ammunition types, the right to carry, the right gun to carry—so many things RKBA people love to discuss. You could even say this book, with all its theories and proposals is just a lot of cold air.

Cold air is easy to spot because it has a grammatical component. Cold air is spoken in the future tense: "If you shoot a guy with a nine, this will happen." Reality comes in past tense: "This guy was shot four times with a nine but he survived because his sport coat deflected the rounds."

A few days before this book went on press I had a chance to chat with a judge who is so high up the food chain that I cannot even imply who the person is. First I described the basic problem this book looks at—relinquishing your rights and unwittingly convicting yourself on a 911 call. The judge expressed surprise, having not thought this through previously, the same as other legal eagles. Then, unprompted, the judge stated, "Well then you should call your lawyer first, and have your lawyer call 911, since your conversation with the lawyer would be privileged and inadmissible."

It gave me a chill to get such an unsolicited affirmation from so high up, and I explained that most lawyers and others rejected it totally for reasons I've described here. This person expressed outrage that a prosecutor might use that against you, saying it would be unethical and simply wrong, since your right to an attorney should be above any other consideration. If your case ever reached this person you'd have an ally, but don't count on it, and don't expect that reaction from many other officials, if my experience in researching all this means anything.

External Support

Among the various experts are a handful of groups dedicated specifically to self defense, discreet carry with and without permits, and collective support for legal representation. Members are assured of initial and rapid legal counsel in the event of a self-defense incident, for the cost of membership.

Perhaps the highest profile group is The Armed Citizens Legal Defense Network (ACLDN). Their website is bursting with the same sort of information you find in this book, though we don't agree on all points, par for the course. Attorney Marty Hayes, who leads the group, has an impressive set of credentials, and has assembled an equally impressive set of experts to pen white papers and editorials on the use of deadly force and its aftershocks.

Some of their points seem to make a lot of sense. Other parts are open to the same sort of attack or skepticism that material in this book makes you wonder about. The very idea, for example, of having what ACLDN calls a "go-directly-to-jail" card in your wallet is "a damning piece of evidence that can be used against you in court." Just Google ACLDN to read more.

On closer examination however, there are no shown examples of such a card being used in court to either positive or negative effect (though I have heard stories of such cards helping at the side of a road). This lack of tangible results has not prevented a number of otherwise successful attorneys from putting statements on the backs of their "get-out-of-jail-free" cards.

One attorney consulting on this book questions the doubts about wallet cards and asks, "Is that just a guess, or do they know of some cases where that happened? Consider the self-promoting blowhard angle." Or maybe just the people-love-to-opine-about-this angle.

The ACLDN website makes compelling points about pre-printed statements, but without concrete examples they are conjecture—the kind I've noted people love to sling around ("cold air"). Could such a card make self defense seem like premeditation, or change a life sentence into a death sentence, or even enable a rookie prosecutor on his first case to nail you, as ACLDN suggests? You get to decide what's in your wallet, and truly concrete advice is not something I could find.

Perhaps, over time, this new idea of a reverse *Miranda* statement in the hands of innocent people will gain more traction than it currently has, police will expect it, courts will recognize it. In any event, having legal eagles behind you as ACLDN provides is a worthwhile alternative for folks who choose not to have an attorney of their own, and could provide a significant cost savings. At least, reading their free posted articles is worth your time.

The Texas-based CHL Protection Plan is something of an outgrowth of the Texas Concealed Handgun Association, and similar other join-now-for-legal-services-you-may-need-later groups. A Google search reveals a number of these which you should examine carefully before joining. President Rick Mackey has done an admirable job of promoting the need for legal counsel right there next to the carry permit in your wallet, and his group has saved the bacon of some of its members. Visit chlpp.com.

The CATO Institute recommends a nice short video, "10 Rules For Dealing With The Police," which they call "a goldmine," according to one of their lead attorneys. The film starts with some wiseass black dude blaring hip-hop "music" during a roadside traffic stop, but at least he gives the cop real bad attitude. He predictably ends up in deep doo. The film's black instructor contrasts that with the same scene and respectful acting, with predictably improved results. Sure, the person did nothing wrong in either case, but that's life. You want to express your anger to the man and feel all oppressed and abused, or earn a smile and hear you're free to go, have a nice day? http://www.cato.org/events/100212screening.html

Flex Your Rights is a website with a lot of good lessons to learn, very much worth a visit on your continuing road to enlightenment: http://www.flexyourrights.org

This group focuses mainly on how to prevent yourself from being deported for being in the country illegally. Some of their advice is very questionable in my mind, but they recommend carrying a card to show, which is

particularly useful if your English is bad:
http://www.borderangels.org/knowyourrights.html

The widely circulated Prof. James Duane video is quite
excellent and eye opening: *Why Innocent People Should
Never Talk To The Police*. Police officer George Bruch's
reply is frighteningly realistic. You want to get out of an
interrogation—but he is getting paid for as long as he
can keep you in it; the best result, the one he seeks, is
one with a confession, which makes him look really good
and makes his boss' job easy. http://tinyurl.com/m3crvs

The defense attorney's big job is to get to you before the
officer does, Bruch says, because you're a stark amateur
and the interviewer is a seasoned pro who *will* get info
from you. His ability for deception, misdirection and sly
tricks is mind boggling (police can legally lie to get you to
talk and he's great at it). If he turns off his tape recorder
and tells you this is off the record for the moment, he
knows the entire room is wired for sound and video, but
you think the tape has stopped—and it gets much worse
than that: http://tinyurl.com/ykkraf7

And finally (though there is more out there), the roll-on-
the-floor-funny Chris Rock skit, *How Not To Get Your
Ass Kicked By The Police* is too poignant and hysterical
to miss: http://www.youtube.com/watch?v=uj0mtxXEGE8

CHAPTER SEVEN
Skeptics

It was surprising to me to see how many lawyers were dead-set against approaches I've outlined here—including the very procedure police deem proper. These attorneys eagerly and easily disregarded the very essence of *Miranda*—*You have the right to remain silent and to have an attorney present.* I'm just suggesting that a *Miranda* approach seems perfectly reasonable—but it puts me against a tsunami of attorney disagreement.

Did you notice how many seem steeped in a statist government-lackey mindset, that insists if you call your lawyer first and remain silent until you can make a non-adrenalized statement, this will and even should be used against you. I think that needs to change. Do those lawyers need re-indoctrination camps to re-instill The American Way? Are those lawyers the lawyers you should seek out? Where are the others?

A few of these "defense attorneys" sounded more like arrogant state prosecutors on a bad day. It hurts to say that but it's true. Like the inquisitors you may have to face, their tone was sort of, "How dare you suggest that we, the mighty state, bow to you after a shooting, you must bow to us!" There was no sense of, "Sir, you are lucky to have survived this heinous criminal assault, thank you for protecting yourself and the community. Is there anything we can do to help you as we cart this habitual-offender parole-violating low-life maggot out of your living room? Would you at least like a glass of water, let me get that for you sir." Let me reconstruct some of the bad attitude for you. Lawyers have written these questions to me, making my job easier.

1. "Alan, it is not realistic to expect that people, especially after a stressful shooting situation, will call their lawyer before they call 911."

That of course is the whole point behind the paradigm shift this book suggests. You (and the lawyers) have been too bombarded with the state's incessant insistence to "Call 911" which is clearly *not* in your best interests after a self defense, and violates the very principles behind *Miranda* from the innocent defendant's point of view. These lawyers may be following the norm, and are court-savvy, but it seems to me that has to change.

People need to re-learn that, if you do have the right to have an attorney present, the safe sequence is "Call your lawyer *immediately* and have your lawyer immediately call 911," in order to protect you, all parties concerned and your precious rights. The despicable criminal who just tried to kill you (again, assuming a proper act of self defense) is *secondary* to you avoiding the electric chair through "justice" gone wrong, IMHO. Lawyers disagree.

The idea that if the innocent just come clean they'll be protected is a pipe dream. And if you're not innocent and do bear some guilt don't worry, justice will be served and you'll get yours. Mebbe.

2. "Indeed, this fact is something that a court or a prosecutor may try to use against them."

No doubt they may try, but attacking an innocent person for calling an attorney seems a humiliating unethical corruption of the system and thwarts justice. If you have a right to an attorney, you have a right to an attorney without delay, and before your situation deepens. Any authority who claims "You only have a right to an attorney later after you make unpredictable high-tension remarks into a police recorder *that will be used against you*," is no legitimate authority in an American scheme of justice, in my opinion.

3. "It could make them appear as if they have no regard for human life."

The *only* person, I say again the *only* person with no regard for human life was the detestable criminal who tried to take your life away and failed. Proper regard for human life—your own and the lethal consequences you could face at the hands of "justice"—now exists on your shoulders for you, and *then* for an injured felony dirtbag who tried to murder you, *in that order*. The bad idea that a defeated homicidal predator deserves greater or faster attention than you do is a twisted distortion of what America stands for. Anyone who holds that notion needs sensitivity training. Again, it hurt me to hear so many attorneys take that point of view. Well, what can you expect from licensed and sanctioned agents of the state.

Yes, of course, any wounded person deserves attention, quickly. But first save and protect the innocent—from physical harm—and legal harm that may be far worse, no?

4. "The lawyer isn't going to call 911 for them."

Then maybe you need a different lawyer? One practitioner went so far as to suggest, "You will never sell this to attorneys... In my opinion, an attorney would be foolish to make such a call. Hope you wanted honest feedback." Fortunately, at least some attorneys disagree with that. Richard Stevens is one, and he says, "Having the lawyer on-scene helps the client by reassuring her that someone is watching her back and is on her side. As all of us know, for a client, that kind of moral support matters a lot."

5. "The lawyer has no way to know anything about the facts."

Your lawyer doesn't need to. "George, I've just been involved in a self-defense shooting and I'm shaking like a leaf. I seem to be OK but I'm not sure. The assailant is down, I hit him four times, center of mass. What should I do?" is sufficient to set the wheels turning, and have a *good* lawyer begin lawyering.

6. "The lawyer would simply be repeating things said by the possible defendant."

That's correct. All the lawyer needs to know is the location. Repeating that to 911 seems perfectly fine and proper to me. It's like shouting, "Someone call 911!" The survivor (hero?) of a tragedy needn't be the one making the call. Don't expect to be treated as or maybe even feel like a hero, but a person who kills a murderer is.

Any statements the lawyer makes about purported facts of the case are not evidence, they are hearsay. The lawyer of course should say nothing like that to 911, and they don't matter anyway, or should not in a system of true justice, which is what we need to get back to if we're not there currently.

Unaffected by massive adrenaline and stratospheric blood pressure, the lawyer should be able to make:

Adnarim Statement Part Two

"Hello, 911? I'm attorney George Victory and my client has just survived an assault. An ambulance and police are needed immediately at location X. I'm enroute there now myself." Click.

That's what a good lawyer should be doing when a client is facing a potentially erroneous murder charge after a self-defense incident, in my opinion. Any jury that uses that against an innocent victim doesn't deserve the honor of being called a jury. This also allows the lawyer to say that she instructed her client not to call 911, putting the onus where it belongs, on counsel, not on the innocent survivor.

7. "This could possibly be used against the defendant."

That should be impossible in a true system of justice. If America doesn't have that now, it needs it. You have the right to remain silent but only *after* you call 911 and record statements for the police? I don't think so. It doesn't say that anywhere. Has a lawyer who argues for that been compromised without even realizing it?

The 911 operators should never dare to impugn this call, and ask, "Why isn't the victim making this call? Who is the victim?" If they do, George Victory should politely say, "I advise all my clients to call me immediately in the event of an emergency. I've got to hang up now and concentrate on my driving."

8. "Additionally, the lawyer could become a witness in the case this way and be conflicted out."

The lawyer is clearly not a witness to the event in any sense of the word. Any conversations between lawyer and client should be strictly privileged communications. If they are not, or if your attorney could somehow be "conflicted out" by conferring, then we the people should *demand* this be corrected immediately.

9. "Being at the scene when the police arrive increases this likelihood."

Balderdash. How many times are the police slower than the pizza delivery? Do you have a right to have a lawyer present prior to any questioning or not? Do you have the skills or composure to handle the police when they arrive? What are you paying your lawyer for? How long are you required to wait for your lawyer to arrive? What if the police are *really* slow and the lawyer isn't—then it's OK? This bad mindset (that your lawyer is supposed to arrive *after* police start grilling you and eating the pizza), or even the next day after your lawyer's restful night's sleep and a shower, needs rethinking I think.

10. "Moreover, what are the chances the lawyer could even get to the scene before the local police?"

Sometimes good, sometimes not. If your lawyer is your neighbor and you both live in the hills, pretty good. Admittedly, in some cases, your attorney's response could be painfully slow for all sorts of legitimate reasons. But then, so are police response times in too many cases. If your lawyer isn't willing to make every effort to get there extremely promptly for a $25,000 retainer and quarter-million-dollar murder-defense case, you need a more motivated attorney. Remember, you're facing a short rope and a long drop. You want a lawyer who recognizes, in advance, the seriousness of this unwanted life-altering tragic disaster.

11. "Now the lawyer is a witness in the case for no reason."

The lawyer has witnessed nothing, and has every right to be there counseling the client when second responders arrive. You have the right to an attorney. You have the right to a team of attorneys. *Immediately*. This should be taught in grade school. Lawyers who think otherwise deserve to be disbarred, or at least go broke for lack of clients. True, this may not make me many lawyer friends, and many do disagree, but it's got to be said.

12. "The lawyer should get dressed and travel to the scene and spend hours of time dealing with the police to be possibly told by the defendant at the end that he has no money to pay the lawyer?"

Only if it's a stupid lawyer and stupid client.

13. "No lawyer will work for free."

Your lawyer isn't expected to. See Chapter Three. In the paid consultation this book recommends, you asked and agreed to an awfully stiff retainer should you need defensive counsel in a potential homicide case. Put it in writing if it makes the lawyer happier. Setting up a trust account is extreme but not out of the question, and should be interest-bearing, inuring to the client.

14. "Do you really expect a lawyer will get out of bed in the middle of the night because someone, who he has no pre-existing relationship with, calls and says he was involved in a shooting?"

Of course not. That's the problem a person *without* a lawyer faces. That's the problem for a person who tells *the police* (the state) "I want *a* lawyer," and who understands nothing of the process, and fired a gun in near total ignorance (but may have saved his innocent life nonetheless; that person, despite possible innocence, is probably screwed blued and tattooed). You on the other hand should be asking a trusted ally you already know to spring to your defense in the darkest hour you will ever face in your entire life. You're also offering this ally buckets of money and one of the most important cases they will likely ever face and get to brag about.

15. "Finally, sleep will be more important to the lawyer when the lawyer has no money placed in a trust account in advance which will usually be the case."

See number four above.

16. "Even where the lawyer does have money in trust and a preexisting relationship, going to the scene may be a big mistake."

It didn't hurt Dick Cheney. "Oh, c'mon, he's the Vice President of the United States." Is justice equal or isn't it? Of course the VP gets some slack. You deserve the same, though comedian Lenny Bruce wasn't too far off when he famously said in his free-speech trial, "In the halls of justice, the only justice is in the halls."

It's impossible to imagine a rich powerful person being harmed by the presence of a team of lawyers and a PI when police arrive. It's actually good for the rich powerful person. Helps keep the authorities in their place, and both sides know it. You've seen the movies. Those exact same protections should exist for the average person who is about to be put in the poor house for defending personal freedom, having just defended innocent life.

The second mortgage, emptied retirement account and poor-house part of the whole self-defense picture stinks to High Heaven, and is among the worst travesties and corruptions of justice in America. Lawyers make their living there, so it should come as no surprise that some hold distinctly un-American views which their system vigorously supports.

17. "Simply telling the police you want to talk to your lawyer works fine."

We agree. Say the magic seven words: "I need to speak to my attorney." *Speaking* to your lawyer though, instead of saying you *want* to speak to your lawyer, is better, no?

18. "Indeed, it is the thing to do."

We agree again, and if your lawyer can't get there first— why, you might be out of town when the incident occurs—asking for your attorney is the thing to do, along with reading authorities your rights in the *Adnarim* statement (or something similar) if needed. Maybe.

If your attorney cannot get there for any reason, or can't even get your phone call, you need *multiple backup phone numbers and contacts*. It's only reasonable. You're facing a gurney and a needle. Is this the time to economize?

19. "I have no issue with having someone else call 911 and generally report the shooting."

If you've listened to any 911 tapes from frantic civilian-involved shootings, you know that *anyone* except the shooter should make the call. A bystander, not a witness, should make the call, to preserve the integrity of the crime scene. "Someone call for an ambulance!" When the pack media gets those tapes and plays them incessantly nationwide for days, after some isolated incident in your home town, there's no reason your voice should be the one that bombards the public. Your voice. Bad idea.

20. "I'm not saying the shooter should give any big statement to the 911 operator. Just make the call."

Ugh, that again. The client should not give *any statement whatsoever* to the 911 operator and voice recorder. None. Your lawyer should *demand* that of you. *You have the right to remain silent.* You get that right when you say, "I need to speak to my attorney." Invoke that. Stand on that. You should exercise this right *without exception*. Anything you say can *and will* be used against you. Haven't you listened to 911 tapes? They are totally incriminating evidence, and are great for turning public opinion against you.

I get a big laugh every time a lawyer advises, "Only say this to 911." Hah. Like you're going to be able to control yourself? Like whatever that poorly trained attorney advised you'll remember? Like 90% of what they advise isn't already incriminating? "Just say you were in fear for your life and that you had no choice and send an ambulance and hang up the phone." Right. Those lawyers need to read this book. And remember, 911 operators are instructed to *demand* that you keep the phone line open. Helps them gather evidence that can *and will* be used against you. And if you hang up they will immediately call you back. *The instant you call 911, they get the phone number and an ID.*

21. "However, do not underestimate the importance of telling the police you want to talk to your lawyer."

We agree. The seven magic words, "I need to speak to my attorney," are powerful medicine, have legal standing, and though the police these days may not constrain themselves by that, those words will help you in court later. Once you "invoke," the legal scene changes, and police know that. It may not stop them, but they know that any further questioning may be ruled inadmissible. Sure, unjust efforts to get you to speak may be ruled out as "reasonably calculated to solicit an incriminating response." At least, if your word stands up to their word.

22. "The police may try to deny the shooter the right to silence. This is a good thing as it allows the attorney to move to dismiss the case later for denying this right."

We agree. I'd change "police may deny this right" to "police typically deny this right" from everything I've heard. Invoke the magic seven words. "I need to speak to my attorney." Protect yourself, even if police ignore it.

23. "There are so many different factual scenarios that anything more than general advice will sometimes be a bad thing."

There is a lot of truth to that, but it cannot replace the need to have some sort of strategy and plan in place ahead of time, just like our friends the police officers do. I said at the get go that changing circumstances are a real problem with a book like this.

> These are general discussions of social issues between American people exercising the right of free speech, to discuss and consider matters of great concern to society. It's an exercise in free speech, not a blueprint for the use of deadly force. This book is not legal advice, and I'm not a lawyer, I'm a First Amendment guy, a writer. Every situation *will* be different. That point has already been made, and the applicability of this book's content to your situation may be a good, bad or a terrible match. *The risks are yours and yours alone.* Remember *that* before you drop the hammer.

Let's be clear about something in America today. If you're black, poorly dressed and caught in a bad part of town, or in a white part of town, all bets are off. If your head is shaved and you have tattoos on it, all bets are off. If you're anything less than a clean-cut white guy in a nice suit and tie with no priors in broad daylight, your odds drop. It shouldn't be that way, but everyone knows it is.

The *L.A. Times* has since 2007 run a homicide blog, and has tracked more than 740 murders, putting faces and names to the bland statistics. While "news" reports were overflowing with stories of Laci Peterson month after month, the paper followed dozens upon dozens of new murders constantly that otherwise got no attention. Their "startling" discovery (for them at least)—almost all of these deaths were young black males.

This reality—so-called "gun deaths" are actually "angry homicides" (their phrase) bound by socioeconomic, geographic and demographic boundaries, has been too horrible for the mainstream to face. *The "news" media generally cooperates to hide the fact that murder has racial and geographic components.* It's easier, more politically correct, and serves a perverse anti-freedom, government-dependency purpose to blame guns and gun owners, than to face an awful truth about our society, and failed social policies that make it that way.

This ugly underverse colors how police and the justice system react, since they cannot ignore it like the misinformed and uninformed public can. It has a tragically negative effect on the right to keep and bear arms. Especially on the use of arms in comparatively rare justifiable homicides, where innocent people walk and guilty ones stop walking. The advice in this book does nothing for the 740 people the *Times* has tracked, many of whose murders are never solved, and who are only discovered, not through a 911 call, but from the smell of a decaying body found in an obscure spot.

24. "Despite the well-known advice not to talk, most people still talk."

Exactly. That's why it seems to make sense to call your lawyer *immediately* in a situation like a successful self defense, when you really really really need your lawyer immediately. Lots of lawyers push the self-contradictory idea that it's crazy to call your lawyer first since you have the right to remain silent. You can't functionally exercise that right and everything is stacked to help you abrogate that right. That's exactly what a lawyer is for. Immediately. The contrary argument that this will go badly with the jury, even if true, is a travesty.

25. "Trying to communicate much more to a client than, 'just shut up' is probably a waste of time and may result in making matters worse."

Just shut up? Stand mute as soon as the round exits the barrel? Or call 911 first and record yourself? Or say the magic seven words? Or read the *Adnarim* statement? Or Ayoob's statement? Read this book and learn. Existing "wisdom" needs heavy-duty re-examination.

Eric Cartridge is a guitar-playing member of my political parody trio The Cartridge Family, and a long-time friend severely knowledgeable in firearms issues and global politics. He makes telling remarks that people too close to the issue simply overlook:

The prosecution has so many advantages over the defense it is insane to refer to what we have as a "justice" system. Here are a just a few: Both the judge and prosecutor work for the state and have a gigantic budget compared to defendants; Defendants must pay $50K–$250K whether they win or lose a criminal trial; Poor defendants are stuck pleading guilty to half the charges the prosecutor can stack against them; Entrapment is now considered a legitimate law-enforcement technique rather than something abhorrent to the Constitution; Prosecutors leverage "confessions" out of people by threatening to indict their spouses, take away their kids, etc. And that's just the stuff that comes immediately to mind.

As an aside—Our current legal system is a joke in terms of meting out justice. Think about this: The prosecution and the judge both work for the State, but the defense attorney is also licensed by the state—and his livelihood will grind to a screeching halt if he doesn't do what the state's judge says in court.

Restrictions on defense attorneys typically include not allowing them to make any arguments the judge doesn't like, particularly those concerning the dreaded "Constitution." The judge lies to the jury and tells them they can only judge the "facts" of the case and not the law (denying fully informed juries). Jurors who do otherwise are threatened with contempt of court and may be jailed. The punishments facing a convicted defendant are kept secret from the jury, even if excessive. How fair is that?

The prosecutor's massive budget is funded by the taxpayers (which includes the defendant!—you pay for your own prosecution) and the prosecutor's office suffers no financial consequences, win or lose. A criminal defendant (if he is very, very lucky!) will spend that quarter million of his own money and be acquitted—you win but you're impoverished. If he is unlucky (which is most likely), he will be convicted... too.

A criminal defendant without money is completely screwed and will be faced with variously inflated "plea bargaining" options designed to prevent the prosecution from ever having to prove its case. The accused can either plead guilty to crime X and get five years, or the state will threaten him with prosecution for crimes Y and Z (known as "charge stacking") which could get him 30 years. In the civilian world, this is know as "blackmail" or "extortion" and it is illegal. In the halls of justice this is known as due process. And it is very effective in filling up prisons with non-violent drug users, by the way.

CHAPTER EIGHT
Good Will

A lot has been said about the need or desirability of getting and maintaining the good will of the responding police, and authorities up and down the chain of command. If you're a wise ass, uncooperative, a know-it-all, belligerent, show an anti-government attitude or you react like you're in some kind of police state, it will go badly for you. It won't matter how innocent your are, or think you are.

If you act on the right to remain silent, the guaranteed, sacrosanct, bedrock of justice, police will very likely assume you have something to hide. That's just the way it is. They often do take the position that if you have nothing to hide then you should just openly confess to everything that went on, and you'll be just fine.

Lawyers of course don't agree with that at all, and say in no uncertain terms, *the police are not your friends*, a point that has been made in this book more than once. They are collecting evidence, not acting as your defense and support team.

Still, if officers take a liking to you, or are convinced early on that you're the good guy and the guy suffering from lead poisoning is the bad guy, this doesn't hurt you. Meeting them at the door and reading a statement from the back of your lawyer's business card may go a long way in killing the good will you might otherwise have.

Former cop Marty Hayes of ACLDN believes that saying nothing and demanding a lawyer is excellent advice—if you're a criminal. The truth will incriminate you, and lies will only make things worse, so shut up.

But police (secretly at least) *love* a citizen who survives by legitimately killing a predator, so police have a vested interest, and a bias in your favor. That's if you can help convince them that: you're innocent, the guy on the ground imitating a victim with bullet holes is the bad guy, and no arrest is needed. If you clam up and demand an attorney you reduce that opportunity.

Once an arrest is made, police have an interest in proving it's a good collar. The crime you truly faced before you fired falls off the burner. Talk about a rock and hard place. Marty's web-posted *Unintended Consequences of Silence* is a chilling eye opener.

California civil-rights attorney and RKBA activist Chuck Michel sums up the mental attitudes that might be best after an incident, based on his 20 years of experience as a prosecutor and defense attorney. Having these in mind might leave you in better standing if and when a court date arrives:

> Your reactions can be twisted by politically inclined authorities, can be misinterpreted by police, prosecutors and juries, and may be understood differently in Texas or Los Angeles.

The appropriate response to being forced to use deadly force to defend yourself is resigned regret and righteous remorse. Not guilt, remorse. As in: "I value all life, even the criminal's; I hated to have to use force that might deprive another person of life, but I had no choice; It's tragic that the guy left me no choice; He forced me to do what I had to do; If I hadn't done what I did, I thought he would kill me."

How to articulate that sentiment unambiguously is the tricky part. I have seen several people, after killing in completely righteous self defense, brake into tears when they see the dead body and realize what they have done. This is understandable, because even taking the life of a dirt bag who deserves shootin' is very, very sad. No matter how righteous, it's sad. But crying can be made to look like you realize you did something wrong, regret your mistake, are upset about it—and this can hurt you.

To avoid feeling that sadness, I have also seen people respond with psychological defense mechanisms, putting up emotional walls and hardening their feelings so they don't feel sorrow for the event or the criminal or second guess themselves and their actions. And you will second guess yourself if you have even a shred of humanity in you.

You will replay the incident in your head and wonder how it might have been different. That response, both the walls and the second guessing can hurt you legally if articulated to authorities because that reaction can also be misconstrued. It can come across as demeaning the criminal, insensitive, and inhumane if it comes across as a casual attitude like "Screw him he got what he deserved I don't care."

As appropriate as that might be in reality, the Dirty Harry tough-guy response is often perceived by a jury, when spun sympathetically by a prosecutor, as cavalier. It can make you look impulsive and trigger happy—you could have avoided the incident but were in a hurry to judge and execute the criminal. Save the self doubt for the psychologist that you should absolutely see if you have to use deadly force, and save the hard-ass self-righteousness for your lawyer in private.

Probably the best reaction is to sit down, say nothing, look sad, and tell them you read a book that said after an incident like this you should say nothing and ask for a lawyer, so that's what you are gonna do. Then ask for the lawyer and say you intend to remain silent. If they keep asking you questions, just keep asking for a lawyer. Don't take the bait. Police are great at getting people to talk, especially after a stressful event. It's natural to want to talk. But in the heat of the moment it's easy to say things that can be taken out of context, misconstrued and spun to make you look like you did something wrong, or worse, that you knew it was wrong when you did it.

There's no way to accurately gauge the value of the supposed good-will phenomenon, or your ability to pull it off, or how it will work in your specific and unique situation. The vast majority of people the police collar and bring in, even if they swear it was self defense, are the lowest of the low, real dirtbags who deserve to be arrested, prosecuted, found guilty, and locked away for a very long time. Police become inured to it. Running into a real self-defense homicide is rare for most of them.

The jury effect is another difficult-to-gauge element of the package. Lawyer after lawyer talked about the effect any of the suggestions in this book (or from elsewhere) might have on a jury. An overwhelming number say a jury will *not* be sympathetic to calling your lawyer first and an ambulance second. That to me represents a total corruption of our system, as I've explained repeatedly, but my angst does not a case make. Every member of the jury should recognize their own terrible risk if they ever have to defend themselves against a murderer, and have complete sympathy and support for calling their own lawyers first, and help for the failed murderer second.

Just because I say your life comes first, possible harm you may have suffered comes first, your safety comes first, your right to remain silent comes first, your right to have a lawyer present when you face possible murder charges comes first after you survive an attempted murder, protection from impending judicial abuse comes first, doesn't make it so. And the lawyers persist. And some of those poorly trained, statist, propagandized, brainwashed and compliant vassals of the state will be your prosecutors, judges and even defense attorneys. Keeping their good will might not hurt anything either.

If the situation is reasonably obvious, if you are panting but alive, shaking from the adrenaline, if you actually do speak and say the right things, and are met by officers who appreciate the Second Amendment and justifiable use of deadly force, and if they decide you're the good guy and this really was self defense, there won't be a jury. If.

No court appearance will be set. The news reports will say (grudgingly) that police think you're lucky to be alive and no charges will be filed. If.

Bottom line is it's a crap shoot. Once again, assuming a perfectly clean shoot, you ought to be able, in a perfect world, to stand on your rights, do the right thing, and have a jury 100% on your side no matter what.

In the real world, all sorts of forces are at play that are not in your interest, and do not serve justice, and have no concern whether you get off or not, and don't care about bankrupting you, and don't particularly like guns or people who have them. You must decide on the trade off between an impregnable don't-say-anything defense, or and *Adnarim* statement, or any other strategy, including being Mr. Nice Guy.

You only have one way to find out which way works, and what the correct steps are every step along the way. That's with your butt on the line, when you make your moves, and later when you either rejoice or regret what went down, and how you maybe could have done things differently. Second guessing will probably stay with you for the rest of your life, win or lose. Maybe then you get to write your book, and question everything in mine.

I thought (foolishly), when I started, that I would arrive at The Answer. Here's what I've learned. There is no answer. Go back and read the boxed comment at the end of Chapter One.

There may however be a policy change going forward, which I only came across as this book neared completion. My brother Richard has an expression I've always found insightful: *Things tend to happen at the end.* Look for that in the conclusion chapter.

CHAPTER NINE
Reporters

Reporters raked vice president Dick Cheney over the coals for not immediately calling reporters and telling them what happened, when he experienced his firearms accident on Saturday afternoon, Feb. 11, 2006. Shows you what reporters know.

No doubt, some of them harbor a secret desire to shoot some lawyer right in the face with a shotgun too.

Calling reporters is the last thing you should do, even (or maybe especially) if you're a public figure involved in a firearms incident. That won't necessarily keep them away though, since they have informants and police scanners and listen in for what they consider juicy leads.

Allow yourself time to appropriately psychologically process your post-shooting psychological trauma, just like police do. Debrief this critical incident for 24 to 48 hours with legally protected personal advisors. Only then should you even consider making a statement to the press, the authorities, or anyone.

A fool makes those statements verbally, because no matter how careful you are anything can come out of your mouth. You don't know what the words will be until they ring out, and you can't take them back any more than you can take back the fired rounds. Reporters are expert at and will press you for more, and it takes a well-composed pro to even ignore their queries and mindlessly repeat, "No comment."

And they can even use *that* against you: "The police shooting suspect (a damning phrase in and of itself) adamantly refused to reply when repeatedly asked why he had shot the helpless young black victim." "Despite numerous attempts to get the alleged perpetrator to speak, he steadfastly maintained an eerie silence." Such common routine bias is disgusting, common and routine.

Anyone with sense *reads* a prepared statement and refuses to respond to belligerent, provocative, deceptive, manipulative, leading, misleading, hostile, antagonistic, generally ignorant questions and insults the biased unethical throng of reporters rudely throw at you, in defiance of your 5th Amendment right against self-incrimination, in an effort to try you before your trial. "No comment" is your friend. Avoid the spotlight.

Expressing sadness, contrition and assuming full responsibility for the incident (as vice president Cheney did in his case) may be appropriate. Working from a written statement prevents the inevitable off-the-cuff remarks that are less than accurate, likely inconsistent and you will surely regret.

Also keep in mind that reporters, as observed in the overwhelming majority of their published work, hate guns, hate gun owners, don't hold much stock in self defense and do not support keeping or bearing arms and righteous programs like discreet carry. I've told them it's not good to hate, but it hasn't helped.

They will sensationalize a shooting incident without fail, and portray it inaccurately. That's just SOP. They're expected to by their handlers. It helps sell papers. They simply do not care if it's ethical or right, and frankly they don't know. They'll argue these facts publicly of course, but their actions speak so loudly you can't hear a word they say. Get a sense of just how bad it is with specific examples from real "news" stories, and see why they're called *stories*: gunlaws.com/NewsAccuracy.htm

One well-known attorney recounts a case where an innocent citizen encountered four gang members at a store, and two tried to rob him. Using a legally possessed firearm, the citizen "took down" one and the others fled. Reporters, hearing of the shooting over a police scanner, raced to the scene. When they learned however, to their dismay, that it was a perfectly justifiable shooting, they left, wanting nothing to do with a valid self defense. Their only interest was in a story that would vilify guns and gun owners. Reporters call this "lack of bias."

"Dr. Michael Brown's" internet-circulated guidelines for reporters covering gun issues says:

> The first principle to remember is that subtle use of terminology can covertly influence the reader. Adjectives should be chosen for maximum anti-gun effect. When describing a gun, attach terms like "automatic," "semi-automatic," "large caliber," "deadly," "high powered," or "powerful." Almost any gun can be described by one or more of these terms. More than two guns should be called an "arsenal."
>
> ... Do not waste words describing criminals who use guns to

commit crimes. Instead of calling them burglar, rapist, murderer, or repeat offender, simply use the term "gunman." This helps the public associate all forms of crime and violence with gun possession...

http://www.gunlaws.com/HowGunSpinIsDone.htm

You have no obligation in law or in policy to speak with reporters if you don't want to, but they'll try to insist otherwise ("If you're innocent, why won't you speak with us?"). Knowing how biased they are on this subject, unless you are fully expert in dealing with them, keeping mum is a good idea. Make it the 187th rule of gun safety—"Don't speak with reporters," out of fear for your own safety. For tips on how to handle a hostile interview:

http://www.gunlaws.com/HostileInterviews.htm

There is a technique that works with reporters though, if you're up to it. *Instead of letting them interview you, you interview them.* This is absolutely not for the novice, but publicists and savvy media experts can pull it off to good effect. Maybe not when you face murder charges, but certainly under other circumstances.

When they ask what happened, or why did you shoot that poor kid, it probably can't hurt you to ask, "Have you been a reporter for a long time?" If they take the bait and fall for that sucker punch, you can continue with your interview for a while before they realize what's happening.

Continue asking curiously (and politely) about their job, to warm things up and keep the subject changed. How did they start, do they like it, have they ever thought about writing a book. Listen. Learn. Show interest. People like it when you show interest in them. Then,

"So tell me, how do you feel about guns?" The answer will likely be a dodge, and a sharp reporter will include a question back, or even chastise you for not immediately answering their question. So you calmly respond by asking, "Do you own a gun, or go to a range to practice?"

Since the answer for most reporters is "no" to both points, the quick followup for you is, "Why not?" Do you see where this is heading? You're taking control and now *they're* getting interrogated.

When they dodge, or ask you to answer or justify yourself or go back to their questions, stand firm and say, "I'm just trying to get to a point," and ask again, "When was the last time you went to a range for practice?"

If you answer *their* questions they can (and typically plan to) use it against you. They can take it out of context, build their own context in the lead-in to color your quote, or just simply make up quotes for you. It happens all the time. It's routine. They deny it, but people who get in the "news" universally experience it. Even *reporters* who get interviewed often express shocked surprise when they get to compare what they said and meant, and what appeared from their peers.

By you interviewing them, you can shed a little light on the situation. You can begin to expose the bias they have but try to conceal and deny. After the preliminary joust, you may actually be able to get them to talk about gun rights, where they stand, whether they think people should be "allowed" to have guns (as if some authority has legitimate power to "allow" you to exercise rights you should be "free" to exercise). Get to one of my favorites, have they ever written stories about the good guns do.

Most get perplexed at that. "What do you mean, *the good* guns do?" They are so transfixed by the comparatively small but way overemphasized criminal misuse of guns, they just don't realize that the proper role of guns is to *protect*. I've been able to go on like this at length, and help reporters (yes help them, which they sorely need), see their biases, unravel the misconceptions they have about guns and gun ownership, and leave them with nothing to report!

I'll even invite them to go to the range, which they typically decline. When we're all done and have said goodbye ("Listen, it's been real nice talking with you but I'm out of time and gotta go, thanks again,") they realize they have nothing in their notes they can use, except their own conflicted, bewildering and generally ignorant sentiments. They realize they've been had. Who was that masked man? Too late.

It's the *Socratic Method*—using questions to help a person understand an issue. I've revealed nothing about myself and provided no useable quotes, but every whopping chunk of stupidity they admitted I turned back on them, to good effect. It's an art, developed over many years of practice. You should catch me in action some time. It's a thing to behold. Works with any anti-gunner willing to talk for a while. I ought to write a book on *that*.

I've completed a white paper on *How To Handle A Hostile Interview*. It's posted at gunlaws.com, under the blue News Accuracy button. That posting has a ton that reveals the true nature of the so-called "news" media—a biased bunch of ignorant elitists who are among the worst enemies this nation faces—and whom you should not face after saving your life.

CHAPTER TEN
The Big Pow Wow

The need to examine the basic paradox in all this—"Call 911, and don't say anything"—moved me to orchestrate a meeting of attorneys and discuss the matter face-to-face. Nine people responded to my call: seven attorneys, a PI and a gun-rights lobbyist, and the ten of us met in the 19th floor conference room at Mike Anthony's law firm, Carson Messinger. Five of the lawyers were full-blown criminal-defense attorneys with long track records, two others have an abiding interest in the subject and are as 2A savvy as anyone you're likely to meet.

We disagreed. The depth of the disagreement surprised me. It seemed to me the irrational rationale of "Just shut up," and "Call 911" would meet with nods of agreement once it was brightly lit. Certainly, the abject elimination of your right to remain silent, and your right to have an attorney present prior to and during questioning, which is eradicated by a 911 call, had to fall once the dots were connected. I could not have been more wrong. The prevailing sentiment among the attorneys to call 911 was adamantine.

The meeting, which I began calling the big pow wow, lasted several hours over dinner and continued by email. The emails preserved in exacting detail the players' own words, replete with all the internal contradictions and disparities, presented here with the parties' permission.

It will raise your eyebrows, and leave you in a quandary from which only you can select your way out.

The discussion began when I circulated a proposed *Adnarim* Statement Part Two, to be made *by your attorney* after you survive an attempted lethal assault:

Adnarim Statement Part Two

"Hello, 911? I'm attorney George Victory and my client has just survived an assault. An ambulance and police are needed at location X. I'm enroute there now myself." Click.

:::

Cast of characters: Attorneys Marc Victor, Thomas Baker, Mike Anthony, Mark Moritz, Richard Stevens, Joey Hamby, Tim Forshey, gun-rights lobbyist Gary Christensen and myself.

Marc: Alan, how does the attorney know the client just survived an assault? What if there are other facts? Another theory? Why lock into one theory now? What does it add for the attorney to go to the scene? How does the attorney know the timing of the event?

Thomas: Alan—Is this an *Adnarim* statement for an attorney? You will never sell this to attorneys for the reasons stated at our meeting. In my opinion, an attorney would be foolish to make such a call. Hope you wanted honest feedback.

Alan: Yes, ruthless support and honest blunt feedback is best by far, very much appreciated, don't stop, even if we disagree on points. Your position is duly noted, and your perspective is well documented in the book. So is the idea that an innocent person is entitled to and is best served by legal representation without delay, *just like police get.*

Many attorneys agree with you, but not all, and from the *client's* perspective, an attorney who will be "present prior to and during any questioning," and one who aids a client in maintaining the much vaunted "right to remain silent," seems to me far superior to the approach most, but not all the attorneys at the pow wow expressed (i.e., leave the client twist in the wind until a convenient-for-the-attorney later time).

Marc: For all of the numerous reasons I discussed at the meeting, I do not believe it is in the client's interest nor do I believe it is in the lawyer's interest to proceed in this manner (make the 911 call or rush to the client's side).

Mike: Alan, solely for the purpose of score keeping (since you see a closer score than I saw at the meeting), I agree with those who do not believe the defense lawyer should make the 911 call and I doubt that the defense lawyer at the crime scene scenario is practical. Yes, yes I know that cop defense attorneys often meet their clients early, sometimes at the crime scene, and I know that citizens should be treated as well as cops, but your book is about reality, not fantasy.

Someone facing a self-defense shooting needs advice that can be used in the real world—don't say anything, don't antagonize the cops (who you hope will include self-defense evidence and witnesses in their reports), recognize that through the process of arrest, booking, investigation, preliminary hearing, bail arrangements, etc., your lawyer will not be with you, and those around you will not be your friends. The self-defense shooter must be strong and resolute.

Mark: Got to concur with Mike. The lawyer who is "on call" at 0300, because you paid him some money once, is a fantasy. With my *mazel*, my lawyer will be in the hospital getting an emergency appendectomy, or her husband will be, or their child will be. Or, I will be in Texas or Utah, while my lawyer is on a trek in Nepal.

What I have chosen for myself is a "support system"— somebody I can call so I can say, "Get me a lawyer," and who I know will then start doing phone calls and emails to find me a lawyer. I've got a few names and numbers of lawyers in my wallet, along with the names and numbers of various family members and two friends (fellow marksmen) whom I know I can call at 0300.

In the meantime, I'd be interested in discussing what to say to a 911 operator, and whether to hang up on the 911 operator. I'm hoping your book will contain first-hand accounts from people who have done this. What did they say to the 911 operator? What did the 911 operator say to them? What did they say to the police? What did the police say to them? What was it like to be arrested? What was it like being in jail? And always, "Me want lawyer," followed by Speaking The Fewest Utterances.

Richard: Well, I'm on call like that for my clients. I was on a plane to Hawaii three hours after learning a client was in a defensive shooting and about to be interviewed by authorities. Same for a case in Kansas City. And I'd be first out of bed if a client were in town here and was caught up in a problem of this sort.

We lawyers high-tail it to arrive in court on time for a freakin' motion or *ex parte* to extend time for a pleading or some other procedural matter. Why would we turn over and hit the snooze button on an existing client who just shot a home invader, is scared out of her wits, and is about to be surrounded by police? I don't get it.

Joey: In the spirit of blunt feedback: I am still very intrigued by Alan's suggestion and I have not heard a specific reason explaining why it won't work.

The criticisms I have heard are:

It is not in the client's best interest. Why not? We all agree that the client should immediately invoke. Why is it in the client's interest to speak to the police on a recorded line immediately after the shooting, when the adrenalin and emotions are at a peak? Why should the client make a call and then invoke? Why not invoke immediately. The one concern seems to be the perception of the investigators, that they will hold that against the client. I can't think of any of my clients who would have been worse off by having an attorney call the police.

It is not in the attorney's best interest. Legal interest or financial interest? Is there a fear that the attorney can somehow be charged with hindering an investigation or being part of the crime? I haven't heard any realistic scenario raising those concerns. The only concern I heard raised is that the attorney will become a witness and will be conflicted off of the case. I guess there are scenarios where that could happen, but if the concern is that the client might confess to the attorney, what is the difference between doing that immediately after the shooting and doing that two days later after the client posts bond and comes to your office? If the only concern is that the attorney might not be able to continue representing the client then that is a risk that has to be factored into the financial arrangement up front and the client has to be made aware of the risk.

An attorney would be foolish to make such a call. Is this different than the last criticism? If so, how?

The attorney will be unavailable at 3 a.m. This is quite possible. However, the fact that Plan A may not work is not a reason to not have one. It is a reason to have Plan B and Plan C.

Clients can be trained to react properly under pressure. I think that is fantasy. (Col. Jeff) Cooper's quote about quarterbacks illustrates this quite well. The citizen client will be a rookie who hasn't played the equivalent of Pop Warner football. Throw them into the NFL and you will simply have a stain on the turf. There are an extraordinarily small number of people who have the natural skills to be able to handle that kind of pressure, even with appropriate training. Going back to the police shooting situations; when a police officer shoots someone they immediately have counsel on the scene. These are the people most likely to be highly trained in shooting, stress management, interrogation, investigation, and testimony, and they don't try to handle it themselves. That should demonstrate the folly of a citizen trying to handle the situation alone.

I am assuming Alan's hypothetical of a righteous, self-defense shooting by an upstanding citizen where the attacker is killed outright. However, if the shooting is less than righteous, it would seem that the immediate need for an attorney is even greater.

Some of the concerns that I have are as follows:

When you have an attacker down and wounded but not immediately dead; in a situation where seconds could make the difference between a murder investigation and an attempted murder investigation, how does the client decide whether to call an attorney or to dial 911 and get medical help? Is the client exposed in some jurisdictions for failing to render aid, either criminal or civil?

I agree with the general perception that Alan's plan will not be well received by the police and that somehow they will try to use that against the client. The question is how, and what will benefit the client the most.

Alan's proposal is a new concept, at least to me. Defense attorneys are generally very averse to new ways of dealing with these situations. Any new idea in this area runs the risk of someone second-guessing you and saying the new idea is crazy because no one else does it that way. There may be legitimate criticisms of Alan's idea, but the criticism that no one does it that way is not a legitimate criticism.

I think we all agree that attorney intervention at the earliest possible moment is in the client's best interest. The question is how early can it happen?

Alan: I'm surprised you still don't get this Marc.

Imagine I'm your client (or anyone else is). Imagine we've already considered the self-defense possibility at length as attorney/client, as my new book suggests and we discussed in the big pow wow at Mike's.

Years later I call you immediately and tell you I just shot some guy who broke in. You need more facts than that to come to my aid, and call 911 so I don't self incriminate? You keep imagining some abject stranger who found you in the phone book. What would you tell *me* on the phone—don't say anything and I'll see you tomorrow after breakfast?

One cop, an interrogator for 20 years, says his job is to question you before your attorney arrives. His skills at deceit and manipulation are tremendous, and all legal, blew my mind (he's on the web). He says "I'm a seasoned pro, you're a rank amateur. I win."

Why on Earth wouldn't an innocent person want an attorney on the scene immediately, if at all possible?

How can you justify, as a client's proper and vigorous defense, showing up leisurely the next day if you can in any way manage to get to the scene—when most needed by the client—without delay?

Marc: Alan, it is not a matter of me, "...not getting it." I simply disagree with you. There is a good reason most criminal-defense attorneys at the meeting also disagree with you. You and I cannot imagine all the factual scenarios that can occur. Maybe you are mistaken about the facts you have reported to me? Maybe you were drunk? Maybe I will generate a different theory than your standard, "My client was just assaulted" theory?

Maybe I am concerned that a jury would find it strange that you called your attorney first before calling an ambulance? Maybe the victim left and an ambulance is not needed? What do you think I am going to do at the scene for you? Why should I chance being a witness to something?

Maybe the victim is preparing another attack and the incident is not over—I may be a necessary witness and possibly conflicted out of the case? Do you really think I am going to get to the scene before police in any event?

There are financial issues too. How much money have you put in my trust account ahead of time to deal with this possibility? Why would you want to park your money in my trust account anyway? Given that you are going to pay lots of money to get me to defend you, do you really want to *waste* your money at $350-$450 per hour to have me get up in the middle of the night to drive to wherever you are in the state and hold your hand for possibly several hours so I can again personally tell you to *just shut up*? Maybe you won't have enough money to pay me for the case?

Given all the possible downside and the fact that the most an attorney is going to be able to do is to tell you to remain silent, I just don't see the value. I would see an attorney who went to the scene as more interested in churning fees than in really helping a client. Apparently, you are not hearing what most of the attorneys around you are saying because you are not getting the answer you want.

Thomas: Alan, Attorneys are not first responders anymore than surgeons are. We are not issued flashing lights and a siren with our bar card. Sure, if an attorney has an existing relationship with a client he may go to the scene for moral support but there isn't go to be any interview or statement from the client following a shooting. Too much emotion and activity to even effectively de-brief on-scene. Nothing more than hand holding going on at the scene.

Clients can be prepared for what to do in advance. Drill it into their heads that the only statement they make is that they have nothing to say without their attorney present. Period, end of law enforcement questioning.

The only person I would send to the scene is a private detective to videotape the scene for witnesses present and/or to preliminarily speak with witnesses. A private detective can later testify at trial, while the attorney cannot unless he is off the case. A private detective can also return to the scene the next day with client's consent to videotape inside home/business. The attorney can go to the scene at that time. The client will be in a better state of mind to debrief a day or two after the incident.

I have yet to hear an attorney state just what they believe they can do at the scene of a shooting. Would they have their client consent to a search of their residence or have law enforcement file an affidavit under oath to obtain a search warrant? Would they subject their client to a law enforcement interview or advise them to invoke their right to counsel and remain silent?

Do they think they can effectively de-brief their client while in the backseat of a patrol car? Do they intend to answer law enforcement's questions on their client's behalf? Just what exactly are the reasons they feel are so important to be there?

What are the specific advantages for the client beyond having the client state, "I will not answer any questions without my lawyer present?" Just what cannot wait until a later date when the client has decompressed for a day or two? Just how is the client "better served" by an attorney being at the scene? Does it really just come down to hand holding?

Marc: I totally agree with Thomas.

Richard: OK, to respond to the question, here is what the lawyer onsite can do:

1. Be someone friendly, reliable and confidential with resources who can help the client with things she needs done after she's taken into custody.

2. Be a second pair of eyes who can keep tabs on the police conduct—potentially reducing overreaching. (This helps my clients for sure.)

3. Give the client reassurance that she, who just shot and maybe killed somebody, is not entirely alone to face the government machinery. (My clients really appreciate this, even if I do nothing else.)

4. Provide a living reminder not to give a statement without counsel present.

5. Be immediately present if a statement is needed, e.g., the dead perp had an accomplice... please describe what happened... which way did the accomplice go... or any other reason for a rapid statement.

There may be other functions and benefits. If I think of them, "I reserve the right to augment my statement."

Gary: This is my non-lawyer's mindset—my attorney is the one and only person with whom I (the 'victim') can speak to *confidentially* and relate something about the incident. I can have my attorney tell the LEOs to go away and leave me (the client) alone, which from so much I've heard, they simply will not do on their own.

At that moment I (the victim) just survived an attack from a "bad guy" and I've long learned—from TV, every CCW instructor I know, and barracks lawyers—that the LEOs are going to try to nail me for *something,* even though it was self defense. The only 'friend' I have left is my attorney. Can't even make a call from jail to say more than, "I need you," since those calls are monitored, recorded, and used to incriminate me the victim. Can't even talk to buddies, wife, or girlfriend without fearing that it will be third-party communication that will be misrepresented in court.

Is that an opportunity for lawyering? Harold Fish spent more than $500,000 to finally get out of prison, after a wrongful conviction and years of pain and suffering on a self defense. You want $400/hr. to hold my hand and quickly lessen that potential? Call it Fish-fear, but every gun owner in my state Arizona is sure that they'll be on the chopping block next. New book title—*Alive But In Jail, The Story Of Self Defense In America*—with a special bonus chapter on how my exorbitantly expensive lawyer stayed in bed while I was being water-boarded.

Whatever happened to the proverbial ambulance-chaser lawyer? Or, is this the result? Image, ethics, or change in the practice? At $400/hr., who can even afford to be defended? I definitely need to charge lawyers more for working on their computer networks. The *Adnarim* approach may not be good legal practice... but it fulfills at least a perception of need if not actual hard-pressed need, and perception is everything.

Alan: Let me add some other obvious things to the list of what the lawyer at your side could do:

The lawyer can say, "Don't answer that," to the client, repeatedly, as police throw one clever leading question after another at the traumatized innocent person ("Is there anything we can do for you sir?" Try not answering *that*). The idea police stop on their own is pure folly. No more questions? They just talk amongst themselves and sweat the victim into incrimination—dialogs that will be missing in the police reports—it's just routine. ("He looks guilty to me, he's being totally uncooperative, I say we run him in and throw in the holding tank.")

The lawyer can say, "We'll work on a statement for you shortly," to the police, as they press the client with every deceptive manipulative tactic in their arsenal. *Delivery* of a written statement can be decided upon later. You want to see how good police are at squeezing info out of you? Watch Virginia Beach police officer George Bruch at a college lecture on the subject, it will make your blood run cold. http://tinyurl.com/ykkraf7

Your lawyer can say, "I want you to stop questioning (or badgering) my client."

The lawyer, if he's good and completely on the client's side, can work to stop the police from booking the client, since *the client has done nothing wrong and committed no crime* (in a clean shoot, or in a shoot the lawyer can position as one that cannot be prosecuted successfully). The client cannot effectively do this alone—but many will feel they must, and start talking to their own detriment. District attorneys maintain their extremely high conviction rates by turning down cases that appear difficult to win. Your lawyer should be positioning your case that way from the get go.

The lawyer, with extensive police experience, can buddy up to the police (might even know them!) and create an air of good will around the situation, to benefit the client. You can't do this alone without making potentially self-incriminating statements, or screwing it up completely.

The lawyer can point out evidence the police miss, a routine and mundane problem, that improves the client's position without requiring the client to make statements or do things that can *and will* be used to gain a conviction in a court of law later.

It's one thing to tell a client "shut up" as has been repeatedly suggested, and another thing for the first responder (the victim/client) to be able to accomplish that with no support structure to lean on in the most traumatized state the person is in or will ever be in. As one interrogator said, "I'm a pro, you're an amateur, I win," after thousands of interviews (see the video linked above).

Recall also Mr. Forshey's admitted inability to control a rant after his witnessing of a non-incident, and again in the conference room as he was leaving. Did you guys not see the result of the 2010 *Thompson* case on *Miranda*

126

rights? Man stays absolutely mute for three hours of intensive police grilling (can *you* do that?), then merely says, "Yes," once, and gets convicted of murder. Sheeesh. And the Supreme Court sanctifies this behavior and result.

The lawyer can be there for admittedly expensive moral support—but support that includes the only ear the client can speak into without creating evidence that can *and will* be used to convict. We know the client will be bursting to speak, and is likely to have some immediate concerns, thoughts, questions, etc., and even quietly making notes can *and will* be used against the client.

The lawyer, on the scene, can help the client's preparation for defense if it will be needed, by gauging the circumstances first hand, and not having to rely on second-hand reports later.

The lawyer can corroborate or contest elements of the police report based on personal observation. Police reports, we all know, can be 'somewhat divergent' from what actually occurred. Man, is *that* an understatement.

The lawyer can direct the PI, part of the client's team who should be present collecting evidence, conducting witness interviews, making drawings, taking pictures, etc. (according to Ayoob and many other experts), which the client cannot do directly without creating evidence that can *and will* be used against the client.

The lawyer can use personal observations later in preparing a wrongful arrest lawsuit to benefit the client and help keep abusive police practices in check.

The truly amazing thing is that there are lawyers who don't already know this, or worse, who argue vehemently against providing immediate support for an innocent client facing the electric chair if the lawyering is faulty. If it's such a bad idea, why do the police themselves obtain immediate lawyering? Riddle me that.

Questions for you:

If a lawyer flatly and truthfully stated to a prospective client, "I will refuse to come to your side immediately after a self-defense incident because I think it's a bad idea," would the lawyer be able to secure the client?

If a lawyer's policy is to refuse to come to the side of a client immediately after a self-defense incident, but fails to disclose this to a prospective self-defense-concerned client, is that righteous or proper?

If a client relies on a lawyer who fails to respond promptly and then suffers harm that would have been averted with a prompt response, does the client have grounds for an action?

These dialogues almost merit their own chapter, to show the public what they face in dealing *with their own attorneys*. I'll gladly do it anonymously, unless some of you on the "I won't come to your side" side are OK being named (which I would *not* do without your permission).

Joey: There are two different concepts that I think are getting mixed up. We all agree that the only thing that should be said is "I refuse to answer any questions without my lawyer present."

Alan's original question was why do we tell our clients that and then tell them to call 911, give a report of the event on a recorded line, and then when the police show up, invoke? That first concept remains a legitimate question and I have not heard a *legal* reason why that could not benefit a client. As best I can recall, my comments have been directed at the issue of having the attorney report the event.

The second concept involves having the attorney respond to the scene of the shooting. I haven't taken a strong position on this issue, other than to say it is an intriguing idea and it is significant that police officers involved in a shooting have counsel on the scene immediately.

I can certainly see some advantages to the client as listed by Alan. I also disagree with Tom and Marc's position that merely invoking is enough in every case and that the police must stop questioning. I would be surprised if they have not had several cases where that piece of law is completely disregarded. I certainly have.

It is much better to not have any statement than to have to make the argument that the client's statement was obtained improperly. Few if any police officers will admit that they disregarded the invocation of right to counsel, overcame a client's will or otherwise violated the law to obtain an incriminating statement.

I am also surprised at the position that there is no benefit to the client for an attorney to go to the scene immediately. I want to go to the scene as soon as possible, when conditions are as close to the way they were at the time of the shooting. If nothing else, it will assist me in preparing the case and cross-examining witnesses. Is it possible that a serious enough difference could occur between what the attorney observes and the police observe so that the attorney might have to testify? That is possible, although unlikely. However, if it does happen, I think the client will be in a much better position by having the testimony than not.

I acknowledge that there can be practical difficulties with both of these concepts. I agree that few clients will have the foresight or the means to retain counsel ahead of time. But I think the concepts are worth exploring.

Also, I may have missed some of the arguments contrary to Alan's proposals, but I don't recall reading anything detailing harm to the client from either of the two concepts. Is there factual or legal harm to the client if the attorney makes the 911 call? Is there factual or legal harm to the client if the attorney goes to the scene immediately?

The one issue that was raised by someone was that you would have to explain to a jury why the 911 call does not come from the client. Could that issue be raised by the prosecution without improperly commenting on the client's right to counsel and privileged communications? Would that get past any hearsay hurdles?

If that is not an issue at trial, what is the harm to the client?

:::

So there you have it. No agreement. "The disparities"— should you call 911 yourself and potentially incriminate yourself, and should your lawyer come to your side as early on as possible, remains unresolved. Marc and Tom make very valid arguments, which I give full credence. Richard and Joey stand their ground against the onslaught and also make good points. I believe I make logical sense, even if the legal community is split about it. Who do you trust?

Marc and Tom I've known for quite a while, and we've enjoyed energetic dialogs over the years. To say we disagree on this topic is a simple truth. Mark and Mike, both very long time and close friends and associates, enlightened the conversation, with both of them pretty much siding with the call-911-yourself school. Richard and I are close personal friends, a man whose legal opinions and social insights have been illuminating to me over the years. It was nice to have at least one philosophically aligned ally in the room.

I met Joey Hamby for the first time that evening, when he arrived as the guest of one of my guests, Bruce Blumberg, who couldn't make it at the last minute. Joey is a criminal-defense attorney in Phoenix, with a primary workload of death-penalty cases. He sat there with little predisposition, pensively weighing the arguments, and came to conclusions that at least partially leaned toward my point of view, a very welcomed port in this storm.

Against the split decision, my own opinion stands that the right to remain silent should be immutable, the Fifth Amendment should be inviolate, the *Miranda* warning should mean what it says, and a person's ability to fairly exercise those rights under stress is known to be so low as to be virtually impossible.

Let it be clear that this is the opinion of one individual, me, a non-lawyer author and proud of it. Some legal experts are adamantly opposed to my opinions. This book is replete with warnings that everyone's opinion is just an opinion, and the only thing that matters is what happens to you when you do whatever it is you're going to do. So be it.

In the interest of fairness, I'll give Marc and Tom the last word—lengthy replies that repeat some of the existing arguments, conflicting stridently with some of the facts and arguments that have come out earlier, that I can easily argue with but won't, and you, dear reader, get to make up your own mind.

:::

Tom: Alan—good discussion. No attorney can provide you a "one size fits all situations" answer for your book. An experienced attorney may be able to sort through the facts of a situation; analyze them in consideration of the applicable law and rules of evidence; and provide a client with a best guess of how a particular situation will pan out. No attorney can guarantee a result even in the most simple and straight-forward situation. The attorney's degree of confidence in the outcome of a case may be high in some cases, but there are always variables that can and do occur.

Without going to extremes, take the following example— a self-defense shooting in an apartment complex. The police are going to be there within five minutes because someone is going to call them. You cannot fire a firearm in an apartment complex without others hearing it and calling 911. The fire department will not come on-scene until the police department has secured the scene. They will stage down the street somewhere regardless of the information given during the 911 call. They may not even respond until the existence of an injured person is verified or reported.

Now, I'll go out on a limb here, and using this simple example, why is the identity of the shooter such a secret? Why the fear of the shooter calling 911 and reporting a shooting and requesting emergency aid? The caller's identity is so easily obtained. The fact that a shooting occurred is so easily obtained. The fact of who fired the shot is also easily obtained. GSR (gun-shot residue) tests will be conducted and roommates/guests have no Fifth Amendment rights—they are witnesses who can be easily subpoenaed before a grand jury. If the person who rented the apartment is present when police arrived, that person is either the shooter or a material witness. Be cautious advocating that witnesses need not co-operate in an investigation—it could, and probably will, be called obstructing an investigation.

How are the benefits associated with non-reporting out weighed by the benefits of reporting? Benefits: shot to stop the perceived threat; immediately called 911 to report shooting and summon police and fire; immediately sought emergency medical treatment for the person because the intent was only to stop the perceived threat, not to kill; and, I suggest to even render aid if possible, or have articulable reasons for not doing so. I know your response to rendering aid, but we are talking about an individual's life and the difference between homicide charges vs. aggravated assault or attempted homicide if the client is in the wrong.

These acts can be argued effectively to support the client's *mens rea* and that the acts were lawful. I do not believe the client is prejudiced in any way. The client does not have to provide a detailed explanation of the events other than those necessary to summon help. I think the issue of just what to say to the 911 dispatcher is what you are looking for.

Assuming that the caller is in fact the shooter, then stating that a shooting has occurred at (location), one person has been shot, and to send police and fire is all that is necessary. If the call is made from a cell phone, the phone will be "locked-up" and unable to make other calls until it has been released by dispatch. Dispatch will immediately call back if the caller hangs up.

When the police arrive it will be a very chaotic scene. They will demand to know where the firearm is; who fired the shot; who else is in the apartment. They will handcuff all those present and conduct a sweep of the apartment. All persons will then be removed from the apartment and then fire department personnel will enter to treat the person who was shot. The police interviews will begin. No attorney could possibly arrive on-scene by this time.

The client either knows about the right to remain silent and to have an attorney present, and refuses to answer any questions without an attorney present, or answers the questions. *Miranda* rights are only required when an individual is "in custody" and is questioned by law enforcement agents. There is a real question of fact and law whether or not the shooter is "in custody" at this point for the purpose of *Miranda* rights. Handcuffs alone are not dispositive.

When the client's attorney arrives, the attorney will not be able to approach the crime scene, i.e., the interior of the apartment, and will be standing behind crime scene tape just like everyone else. Sure, at some time the lawyer will be able to speak with client, but the client has been on their own for, oh, 30–60 minutes? If incriminatory statements were to be made, they have been made by this time.

Let's stay with this simple example, don't change the facts, and tell me why attorney's appearance at the crime scene is so critical to defending client's interests and how it will change the facts or law. I understand moral support, and don't mean to discount it. But how is the client better off than by simply invoking the right to counsel that night?

Marc: I completely agree with everything Thomas said here. This is just the way it goes. The shooter's simple 911 call in this example doesn't hurt the shooter/client at all and allows the lawyer to argue lots about client's *mens rea*. Having the lawyer be the first call (the fact of such call may be admissible) simply looks bad for the jury, causes unnecessary delay and may cause the injured person to die.

What if the shooter was in error? I don't want to be misunderstood either. I agree with Joey about the value of going to the scene at some point. However, I think going to the scene is best after getting the evidence, including witness statements. I have had several cases where the police have continued to question after the invocation. In the cases where this has occurred, I have had suppression motions granted. I have never once had a client who invoked, was then pressured to talk by the police and then uttered a damaging statement that was used against him.

I have had officers who have legally ignored my assertion of my client's right to remain silent and have attempted to question the client nonetheless until the client invoked their rights for themselves. Beyond a stern reminder on the telephone to shut up, there really isn't much an attorney can do at the scene. What small things we can do for clients at the scene are outweighed by the financial costs and legal risks.

Alan, it occurs to me that you don't understand the law regarding questioning after a person invokes their rights. This may explain some of why we do not agree on this point. After a person invokes the right to remain silent by demanding the presence of a lawyer for questioning, the police are not allowed to continue to ask any other questions. This is where the "reasonably calculated to elicit an incriminating response" language comes from. If the police engage in such interrogation after the person invokes one time, any statements are suppressed.

This is different if the person blurts out statements or requests to talk. Again, simply invoking once and remaining silent solves many of the issues you raise. "We will have a statement ready for you shortly" may not be the case. Why do this? Any statement I issue (and I probably won't issue any statement at all) will be after all the evidence is known; not shortly.

The decision to book a suspect or not is not likely to be made by the officer on scene. Usually, a supervisor will make that decision. That discussion is on the phone, even if at the scene. I have personally successfully negotiated a "no arrest" with a supervisor who was not on scene after such a shooting, all from my private office where I have easy access to research, criminal rules, evidence rules etc., and all at much lower expense to the client too.

The lawyer pointing out evidence is ridiculous. We are not investigators. We are attorneys. We won't likely be permitted to walk through the scene while it is being processed in any event. Again, do you really want to make your lawyer into a witness about the evidence at the scene? What was there? Where was it found?

Most murder or manslaughter defendants have a difficult time affording representation at all. Having the attorney on scene for moral support as you suggest at $350/hr. or much more is foolish. The defense is prepared over several months, long after the shooting, when all the evidence is in. It is not prepared at the scene immediately after the shooting. The shooting has already occurred. The witnesses have already seen and heard or not seen or heard what occurred. Gauging the circumstances after the shooting is unlikely to be helpful.

Your comments about the lawyer corroborating or contesting elements of the police report based on personal observation is the exact type of thing I have been pointing out to you repeatedly that can cause the lawyer to be conflicted out. Apparently, you simply don't understand what I am saying here. If you prefer your lawyer to be a witness in your case rather than an advocate for you in court, convince the attorney to come hold your hand at the scene for moral support—to tell you over and over again to shut up.

I actually don't have an issue with the lawyer's PI going to the scene. However, I'm not sure just how helpful it will be and it may cause you to lose your right to an interview later when all the evidence is in. On the other hand, maybe *he* can hold your hand for moral support.

You suggest it is "amazing" that the lawyers do not know all your reasons for going to the scene. At risk of speaking for the majority of my fellow criminal-defense lawyers who would agree with me, we get it. *We do not agree with you.* If you think you know better than the criminal-defense attorneys who practice in this area every day, feel free to give people bad advice in your book.

However, please, in the spirit of full disclosure, do not write that we don't understand your points. I'm all in favor of immediate support. However, going to the scene is not something that is likely to help the client—even if you can envision some strange construction of the facts where it does. There are other lawyer-like things we can do that will absolutely help that have nothing to do with going to the scene.

I believe a lawyer who explains *why* he isn't going to the scene after a shooting can nonetheless secure lots of clients to actually represent in court where lawyers work. I don't think clients expect their lawyers to rush to the scene after a shooting. In my 15 years, I have never been asked to come to the scene after a shooting. If a client really wants a lawyer to rush to the scene after a shooting and can find a lawyer willing to do so, the fee agreement should specifically state what is expected.

I suspect the client will have a change of mind after seeing the fee. I'm wondering how many people want to park ten to twenty thousand dollars in a lawyer's trust account for several years on the very slim chance that they will be involved in a shooting. It isn't going to happen very often. As such, this entire discussion is moot.

It seems Joey is willing to go to the scene after a shooting. I wonder how many people will put money in Joey's trust account just in case. Maybe I will be wrong. Joey, please let me know when you have a mere ten people who have decided to park money in your account for such a purpose. Until then, people involved in a shooting can still call me so I can remind them to shut up over the phone. I will use their money wisely to defend them rather than to hold their hand at the scene.

Tom: Alan - I'm in agreement with Marc. I had never met Marc prior to our pow wow but I hope you take notice that two experienced criminal-defense attorneys have strong view points different than your own. We have been there and done that—lived the real-life experiences involving these issues. No one has ever ended up, nor will they end up, in the electric chair following a shooting you describe because their attorney would not respond immediately to the scene of a "righteous" shooting.

Most of the time no arrest is made at the scene. The DR's (department reports) are submitted to the prosecutor for review and filing of charges. Sometimes an arrest is made at a later date—after the attorney and client have had ample opportunity to meet and discuss. An attorney can do a lot during this period of time.

(Some agencies refer to *incident reports*, or the surprisingly presumptive *offense reports*; these are sent to the prosecuting authority who reviews them and decides what to do. They can pass or decline to file charges, i.e. a direct complaint or grand jury indictment; file on the charges requested by law enforcement; file on a lesser offense or a different offense; or return the case with a request for further investigation.)

I learned a long time ago that only the police own the crime scene. An attorney can only own the courtroom. The courtroom and pre-trial work by an attorney is where the client needs representation. I too will reiterate that the right to remain silent and the right to have an attorney present for questioning are separate rights.

Mr. Thompkins should have simply invoked his right to counsel [*Thompkins* was the recent case referred to earlier, where a single word led to the man's conviction for murder, upheld by the U.S. Supreme Court]. His statement would not then have been admissible. Read the U.S. Supreme Court opinion (syllabus section if nothing else, *Berghuis v. Thompkins*, 08-1470, decided 6/1/10). You need to understand that invoking your right to counsel stops the questioning or interrogation. Period.

Mr. Thompkins did not invoke his right to counsel. He just sat there. No implied invocation was found—it has to be an expressed invocation, an unambiguous invocation. I do not believe that Mr. Fish invoked either [an Arizona self-defense defendant who spent three years in jail and a small fortune before being freed]. The phrase "I refuse to answer any questions without my attorney being present" should be printed at the top and bottom of every page of your book.

CHAPTER ELEVEN
Questions for your attorney

As we've already established, at the same time you buy a ton of ammo and stash a gun in every room of your home, you should "get" a lawyer. When you meet for your paid consultation, you need to ask as many relevant questions as you can, to make sure you have the right person, and to help cement your relationship. These questions provide some guidance for the task.

So, what are the justification standards in this state?

Justification is the legal framework that sanctions, or "justifies" the use of deadly force in a dire emergency. The basic precepts are the same nationwide, but the states have adopted some varying positions. The fundamentals go back for at least centuries, and have been spelled out by the U.S. Supreme Court in a series of 14 cases mainly from the 1890s, which can be found in the book *Supreme Court Gun Cases* at gunlaws.com.

One interesting state-by-state difference is the "reasonable person" standard. The act has to appear to be reasonable, but from whose perspective? In some states it means you honestly believed it was reasonable at the moment you acted (among many other factors). In other states, a third person would have to believe the act was reasonable. This comes down to the jury, who in the first case must decide if they think you believed you were being reasonable. In the second case, it is the jury

141

members who must come to believe that your act was a reasonable one. It's a subtle but important distinction.

Among other factors along with reasonable belief are grounds for belief, actor's innocence, actions not words (provocation), necessity, immediacy, immediacy ends, commensurate force, rightfully armed, mutual combat, wounding, withdrawal, retreat and chase. These were covered by the Supreme Court, and are only the tip of the iceberg.

What sort of experience do you have with firearms?

Have you personally handled a self-defense shooting case before? Tell me about it.

Very few lawyers, even criminal-defense attorneys, actually have a lot of this experience. Many will gain it from your case if you're unlucky enough to ever need their help. The small percentage who do have experience representing shooters typically represent two types of people. First are bad guys who have been caught and are guilty, and the attorney's job is essentially an attempt to lower sentencing.

The other group are people who foolishly use a gun improperly and get into a lot of trouble they never expected and to some extent perhaps didn't deserve (brandishing, pointing, threatening, unintended discharge, prohibited-place carry, unjustifiable shots fired, visible carry where concealment is required or vice versa, etc.). Statistically this is a more likely problem you'll face than an actual armed confrontation.

Let's say I was involved in a perfectly clean shoot against a home invader in my own home. What should I do?

This question is a litmus test. Listen hard. See how the lawyer's response comports with the things you learned in this book and elsewhere, including your own common sense.

What would be different if the incident occurred outside my home out in public somewhere?

If I were involved in a self-defense shooting, what sort of retainer would you expect to begin representing me?

What sort of total cost might be involved?

A lawyer can't give you a really straight answer to this until after the IA, the initial appearance in court. If a low-level misdemeanor is all you're charged with, or if authorities are convinced it's a perfectly clean shoot, an hourly rate or small fixed fee might be proper, and there might be no court appearance at all. If you face a murder charge or other serious felony, your life's on the line and the sky's the limit.

Are there other attorneys you might call in to consult if needed? Tell me about them.

A lawyer who has successfully defended an innocent citizen involved in a difficult defense case will have sky-high rates, and might be the best choice if money were no object. Since money is an object (a mortgage on your home is only worth so much) such an attorney can be used as a specialist, while your attorney handles the brunt of the legwork, filings and preparations.

The Big Q: If I ever have to act in self defense, my own life could be in jeopardy afterwards in court. Are you willing to come to my defense immediately afterwards if you can?

Almost all of the attorneys I spoke with said they are *unwilling* to make such a commitment. They argued vigorously that it's a bad idea from a legal standpoint (though most of those excuses, found in Chapter 7, seemed unjust or illogical to me, or emphasized a corrupt nature to the system; that debate continued with vigor in Chapter 10). They pointed out, quite rightly, that they might be in court or handling some other client's desperate need (and didn't suggest there should be some sort of backup plan for that very reasonable problem). They were perfectly comfortable letting you fend for yourself at the scene (where I think you need your lawyer most). They said "Say nothing except 'I want to speak to my attorney,'" (who isn't here and doesn't want to be). They would trust you to say nothing else until they bail you out in the morning at a decent hour. They're content to let you go through your hour of greatest need alone, and trust that you can keep your mouth shut, which you can't even do in a bar when you're not being grilled. How happy are you with that as a plan? Me, I'd like my hand held. And my mouthpiece present.

Many blew cold air, imagining the emergency call was from a stranger, a non-client, a possible criminal since many shooters are, filled with unknowns and no trust factor, making response impossible. They also acknowledged that without significant funds already in a trust account, they can't begin to start lawyering on the caller's behalf. One even admitted that he was entirely averse to having his own name appear in the police report, so staying away was preferable. For all the lawyers I've dealt with on this project, *not one* expressed having or wanting a relationship with a client that was sufficiently robust to jump to the person's side in the darkest hour of need. The only exception—in stark contrast to the lawyers' approach—were the self-defense organizations, where part of the promise to members is immediate representation.

How long after an incident might I have to wait until I could be represented by counsel?

What do you recommend I do while waiting for you?

Is there another attorney in your firm who might be dispatched to the scene if you were unavailable?

If yes, ask to meet this person.

Do you have a private investigator on staff, or is there a firm you regularly use when you need to collect evidence?

Have you followed the *Heller* or *McDonald* cases?

Heller is the Supreme Court case that established the right to keep and bear arms as a "specific enumerated right," at least for a handgun at home for personal self defense; *McDonald* asked if states are obligated to honor the Second Amendment rights of the people, and the Court said yes, with qualifications.

What are your thoughts on *fully informed juries*?

You should surf the web for information on this important subject. This is a jury's duty to examine both the facts of a case, to determine guilt or innocence, and the law a person is charged under, to determine fairness. Many lawyers, and most judges and officials believe a fully informed jury is a bad thing, and prefer to refer to it by the pejorative and demeaning term *jury nullification* (from the fact that a jury can return a not-guilty verdict if they feel the law in question is unjust).

Nullification however is a bulwark of freedom this nation was built upon. Google, e.g., John Peter Zenger. When legislatures enact laws that are fundamentally bad (like imprisoning people who help slaves gain their freedom), a jury of your peers is supposed to refuse to convict because the law is unjust. It is the ultimate, and indeed the only, functional check on a corrupt legislature, or laws that go against the grain of the human and American spirit. Judges frequently refuse to let juries know they have this power in the sanctity of the jury room, to help obtain verdicts judges want. A prospective juror who admits to supporting fully informed juries will not be impaneled in almost all cases, one of the greatest current abuses of the justice system in America.

What are your thoughts about constitutional defenses?

Many judges refuse to allow defenses based on constitutional guarantees, as irrational as that sounds. Many lawyers will play along with that, for fear of angering the court or just losing the case on procedural grounds. Courts prefer to use precedents and modern rules, which are frequently in direct opposition to the Constitution, to gain convictions. Defendants, seeking to get off, would often like to argue that the Constitution exonerates them, but courts have grown immune or even hostile to that.

If my case were to attract media attention, would you help in managing any public relations aspects, and bring in professionals to help shape popular opinion?

Often overlooked but an important facet of self defense, the media usually runs wild and without constraints in shooting incidents, making things up as they go. Don't expect a lawyer to have this covered. A PR expert can work to ameliorate or even use this in your favor since, after all, an innocent victim has survived and a malicious predator has been legally stopped. I've got to tell you though—most lawyers are completely unprepared for such an insightful, probing and intelligent question, and will pile on the snow job so watch out.

What kind of fees am I looking at?

When it's all over and I walk away a free man, can we go out for a good steak dinner, or to the range, to celebrate?

Questions for your attorney

CHAPTER TWELVE

The Limited Immunity Solution
and maybe a good jury instruction too

You learn a lot when you write a book. In learning about and examining the paradoxes and injustices of the aftermath of self defense, I've come to some conclusions.

Failure to call 911 after a successful self defense, at least in our present state of judicial disarray, can and probably will be used against an innocent person to imply guilt. Such an implication is immoral, unjust, and conflicts with protection of the innocent, but it's not going to change by itself in the near term (though it badly needs to be reversed).

Defense attorneys report that a significant percent of convictions in self-defense cases rely on traumatized and frantic calls to 911 made by the victim of the assault, who survived the mortal combat. That's just wrong.

Calling 911 does unquestionably abrogate your nearly sacred rights to remain silent, to have an attorney present during questioning, and to refuse to do anything that might tend to incriminate you. Even though there is no legal obligation to call 911, you are expected to do so and relinquish your rights. This is bad.

It's not uncommon for the heroic innocent survivor of a lethal assault to think (along with a big chunk of society!), at least internally, "I hope that sombitch dies." A decent respect for your own humanity however, and certainly the legal framework in this country, requires you to suppress such thoughts, at least publicly. Failure to do so can have grave consequences unprotected by any sense of free speech, that's for sure.

A surviving murderer who failed and is shot full of holes in the process (or any attempted rapist, armed robber or similar scoundrel) deserves prompt medical attention, so a call to the state ambulance provider, at taxpayer expense, is not an unreasonable expectation. At the least, this can turn the innocent person's defensive posture from fighting a murder charge to something less, even though police and other experts very often gloat that the dead cannot fabricate lies or testify against you.

So although I firmly believe that, *in theory*, the proper action for an innocent person to take is to preserve your rights by calling your attorney, speak candidly, and have your attorney call 911 *immediately*, it may be prudent to call 911 yourself. Give up your right to remain silent. Give up your right to an attorney. Give up or possibly compromise your constitutional protection against self incrimination. Call 911 quickly and: 1–firmly establish that *you* are the victim, and 2–that help is need immediately, by saying:

Adnarim Statement Part Three
Ten words for 911

**"I've just been attacked.
Send an ambulance and police to (location)."**
Then hang up, call your lawyer, and wait.

Another solution to the dilemma, elegant in its simplicity and perhaps better, is obvious after your see it, but was missed throughout the bulk of the work on this book:

The state should provide limited immunity to anyone who calls 911 in good faith for the purpose of truthfully reporting a self-defense incident and requesting emergency assistance.

The state has a serious vested interest in encouraging its citizens to promptly report encounters with criminal elements. Fear of entanglements for making such calls likely reduces such desirable activity. A simple statute could alleviate this problem to everyone's benefit.

Phoenix criminal-defense attorney Thomas Baker (who has been a tremendous resource in developing this book) suggested this approach, and did the first draft. I cleaned it up just a bit, took out the Arizona-specific parts, and present it here as model legislation for anyone in a 911 calling area. (You may recall from earlier that 911 is an optional service, cities and counties pay a lot to provide it, and some places don't have it and don't even want it, but that's another story.) We should also note that this is not wholly new law—airline pilots fought for and got immunity for cockpit recordings, and police routinely have immunity during IA investigations, both reasonable common-sense protections for the innocent.

Model Legislation

LIMITED IMMUNITY FOR STATEMENTS MADE WHILE REPORTING THREATENED OR ACTUAL USE OF PHYSICAL OR DEADLY PHYSICAL FORCE IN JUSTIFIABLE SELF DEFENSE.

(a) Any individual who is directly or indirectly involved in an incident involving the threatened or actual use of justifiable physical or deadly physical force shall be granted limited immunity for all statements made in a good faith effort to promptly report such incident to the appropriate authorities in an effort to obtain emergency medical or law-enforcement assistance.

(b) The term "limited immunity" shall mean that no statement(s) made by an individual in a good faith effort to promptly report an incident involving the threatened or actual use of justifiable physical or deadly physical force may be used against that individual in any civil or criminal proceeding. [Other terms defined as necessary.]

(c) This grant of limited immunity shall not apply to the prosecution of false reporting, obstruction of justice, tampering with evidence or perjury.

(d) The contents of a report made to promptly report an incident involving the threatened or actual use of justifiable physical or deadly physical force, in a good faith effort to obtain emergency medical or law-enforcement assistance, shall not be released to the public or the news media prior to its use in a trial involving any such incident.

:::

Prosecutors and others will no doubt object wildly to this, claiming they'll never again be able to convict criminals if such a law passes. Balderdash. They made that argument when the *Miranda* warning went into effect, yet they still manage to convict more than 90% of the cases that come their way. It simply means they have to *work* to get convictions, not sit back and let innocent people unwittingly convict themselves on a telephone.

Attorney Baker also included a legislative Statement of Intent to go along with the draft language, which I've fine tuned just slightly below:

Whereas the state legislature has enacted legislation defining certain circumstances in which a person may lawfully threaten to use or actually use physical or deadly physical force;

Whereas the state legislature recognizes a value in having justifiable instances of threatened use or actual use of physical or deadly physical force promptly reported to the appropriate authorities to assist in the prompt dispatching of emergency medical and law-enforcement personnel;

Whereas the state legislature recognizes that individuals who threaten or use justifiable physical or deadly physical force have a deeply rooted constitutional guarantee against self incrimination, a right to remain silent, and the right to have an attorney present prior to and during the course of any potentially criminal investigation;

Whereas the state legislature desires to strike a balance between the potentially competing needs for prompt reporting of such incidents and an individual's constitutional right to remain silent, have an attorney present prior to and during questioning, and be protected from self incrimination, all of which could legitimately delay prompt reporting;

Therefore, the state legislature hereby enacts the following statute to provide limited immunity to individuals who are directly or indirectly involved in an incident involving the threatened or actual use of physical or deadly physical force if they promptly report such instances by calling 911 or other appropriate authorities.

:::

And finally, a proposed "teeth" clause, which I believe many laws need to have, to control authorities, officers, politicians, employees, bureaucrats and other "officials" who frequently and with impunity violate laws and emerge unscathed:

"(e) Anyone who violates or attempts to violate the immunity provided in subsection (a) of this section, or acts in violation of subsection (d) of this section, shall be subject to prosecution as a class 1 misdemeanor for a first offense, a class 6 felony for a second offense, and a class 5 felony for any additional offenses, whether or not additional offenses are committed against the same or different persons, or related to the same or different cases, and regardless of the jurisdiction in which the violation or attempted violation occurs, or time that may pass between subsequent violations."

This is modeled after the highly successful *Posse Comitatus* federal law (18 USC §1385). Instead of saying, as so many federal laws do (paraphrasing here), "It's illegal to use the military to enforce civilian law," which would be toothless against an offender, the statute says, "Anyone who uses the military to enforce civilian law shall go to prison for a long time and pay a very stiff fine." That difference, and people's unwillingness to suffer those enumerated consequences, is why America is not a banana republic.

A movement to get similarly biting teeth attached to numerous other laws already on the books would sure get my vote.

:::

For the final Defense-Of-The-Innocent icing on this cake, Phoenix attorney Steve Twist has suggested introducing a jury instruction in appropriate self-defense cases.

Although few such cases actually make it to jury trial— the vast majority are dismissed for lack of evidence, apparent lack of criminal wrongdoing, difficulty to successfully prosecute or in the best interests of justice— the few innocents who are brought to trial deserve the benefit of robust protection against unintended self incrimination and adrenaline-fueled poorly chosen language in a 911 call which *de facto* abrogates the right to remain silent and have a lawyer present.

Common law has tended to treat "excited utterances" as reliable statements, even when presented as hearsay. But as 911 call after 911 call shows, it's just not so, and is clearly open to serious challenge—bad word choices, emotional and inaccurate chronologies, inconsistent retellings, desperate screams, intentional deception, scrambled sentences, even grossly incorrect baseline facts should prompt a court to warn a jury. "As a matter of law, statements relating to self defense made immediately after surviving an attempted mortal assault are known to be highly suspect as far as accuracy and reliability are concerned." Let the expert witnesses duke it out over that.

A jury instruction should come from the judiciary, in response to laws enacted by the state legislature. They'll have to devise, design and divine the language. That law, about limited immunity for 911 calls, needs to be passed without delay. Then the judges of this land need to step forward and do what's right to protect the innocent, and make our precious Fifth Amendment protection against self incrimination a shining example of exactly what's right in America.

AFTERWORD

Libertarian attorney and former Marine Marc Victor's business card got me thinking about all this years ago. He put a bold statement on the back of his card that his clients could read to an officer who detains them, if the officer went fishing and asked for consent to a search.

Everyone grooved on the language—we were socking it to the man, at least in our imagination. People reveled in reading this riot act—to friends. Me too. Is a clever card a serious factor in a real self defense?

Consensual searches are generally a bad idea for an innocent person, but people are often intimidated into consenting by officers who ask (and many officers are good at intimidating to get that result). It's hard to say "No" when a uniformed armed officer in your face wants to search you or your vehicle. Hence, the card as an ally.

Marc and I discussed this over the years. I tried to motivate him to change the statement, make it more clear (to me at least), and broaden it, but time and tide worked against us. It was such a good first step, and I admired him for his gutsiness in putting it there. I had not seen another lawyer do this. I believe many should. I meet tons of lawyers.

It made me think about an underlying principle. *Why would we accept the state telling us what our rights are?* Did the U.S. Supreme Court in *Miranda* get that backwards? Did the state get a new power it should not have, in the name of protecting us—and we all missed it? In the grand tradition of the Declaration of Independence and the Bill of Rights, *we* should be telling *them* what our rights are, no?

In the context of a traffic stop, or especially in a self defense incident— you and I should want the police put on notice that they damn well better be careful in handling us. Maybe this is your lawyer's job, or maybe the task falls to you. Clothed in righteous innocence, wouldn't you want a statement to convey this sense of things:

"Officer, I understand you face a tough situation here, but please remain keenly aware that self defense is a perfectly justifiable activity embraced by society, it saves innocent lives and is not a crime, and I am not to be treated as a criminal.

"While you must deal with some of the worst elements of society in your duties, that is not the case here. I am an upstanding member of the community with no prior criminal record and have just saved myself or another innocent person from a vicious felonious assault, and it is your sacred duty to serve and protect me.

"My intention is to cooperate with you. Please understand that if you act in any way that compromises my rights or freedom outside the due process of law, I will defend myself from your actions. While I understand that your legal protections are robust, as they should be, so are mine. Your legal veil is not absolute and you are not beyond reproach, so please do everything in your power to avoid forcing me to take legal actions against you personally, your department and the city or agency that employs you. Let us work together to dispose of this matter as swiftly as possible, put the criminal perpetrator in a prison or morgue, and get on with our lives. Thank you for your cooperation. Do you understand the statement I have just read to you?"

Right. That'll never happen, but there it is. And it's easy to imagine pundits, authorities, judicial officers and attorneys taking great offense at that approach (yes, I'm understating it). But I can also imagine great cheering and heartfelt thanks from the teeming masses yearning to be free, wishing it were exactly so.

The American Way is that, "The people are the sovereigns, and the state is the servant." That principle should be held in highest regard when a member of the community is compelled to use or threaten force in defense of life, liberty or property. A lawyer's highest role, and indeed the state's, includes working to serve that principle of personal sovereignty. That's why Marc's card was so poignant, and why it made me think so deeply on all of this.

It came as a surprise then, when in developing this book, so many defense attorneys expressed the exact opposite of those principles. Some of those responses could have been written by arrogant state prosecutors on a bad day, and are captured in these pages for all to see. My hope is that the individuals, whose knee-jerk gut reaction is to castigate the innocent seeking to protect themselves, will read this book, see the error of their ways, and support a change of policy, predilection and mindset in the judiciary.

At a bare minimum, there is no sound reason against championing limited immunity for calling 911, or a jury instruction that protects the innocent who make such a call in a traumatized manner, and fail to protect their right to remain silent, have an attorney present, and exercise the Fifth Amendment protection against self incrimination.

About Alan Korwin

Alan Korwin, the author of five books and co-author of eight others, is a full-time freelance writer, consultant, speaker and businessman with a twenty-five-year track record. He is a founder and two-term past president of the Arizona Book Publishing Association, which has presented him with its Visionary Leadership award, named in his honor, the Korwin Award. He has received national awards for his publicity work as a member of the Society for Technical Communication, and is a past board member of the Arizona chapter of the Society of Professional Journalists.

Mr. Korwin wrote the business plan that raised $5 million in venture capital and launched the in-flight catalog *SkyMall;* he did the publicity for Pulitzer Prize cartoonist Steve Benson's fourth book; working with American Express, he wrote the strategic plan that defined their worldwide telecommunications strategy for the 1990s; and he had a hand in developing ASPED, Arizona's economic strategic plan. Korwin's writing appears nationally regularly.

Korwin turned his first book, *The Arizona Gun Owner's Guide,* into a self-published best-seller, now in its 24th edition. With his wife Cheryl he operates Bloomfield Press, the largest publisher and distributor of gun-law books in the country. It is built around nine books he has completed on the topic, including unabridged federal guides *Gun Laws of America* and *Supreme Court Gun Cases,* a large line of related books and DVDs, and nearly 1,000 radio and TV appearances. He was an invited guest at the U.S. Supreme Court for oral argument in *D.C. v. Heller,* which led to his 11th book, *The Heller Case: Gun Rights Affirmed. After You Shoot* is his 13th book.

Alan Korwin is originally from New York City, where his clients included IBM, AT&T, NYNEX and others, many with real names. He is a pretty good guitarist and singer, with a penchant for parody (his current band is The Cartridge Family). In 1986, finally married, he moved to the Valley of the Sun. It was a joyful and successful move.

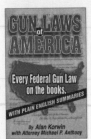

Published by
BLOOMFIELD PRESS